Practice
of MAGIC

Practice
of MAGIC

An Introductory Guide to the Art

Draja Mickaharic

SAMUEL WEISER, INC.

York Beach, Maine

First published in 1995 by
Samuel Weiser, Inc.
P. O. Box 612
York Beach, ME 03910-0612

Library of Congress Cataloging-in-Publication Data

Mickaharic, Draja.
    The practice of magic : an introductory guide to
the art / Draja Mickaharic.
        p.   cm.
    Includes bibliographical references and index.
    1. Magic.   I. Title.
    BF1611.M53   1995
    133.4'3 – dc20   94-49078
                                                       CIP

ISBN 0-87728-807-0
CCP

Cover art by Nieto. Courtesy Walter Holl Agency,
Germany.

Typeset in 11 point Palatino

Printed in the United States of America

00 99 98 97
10 9 8 7 6 5 4 3 2

Table of Contents

Introduction

People who learn magic learn it in the same way we learn about any other technical field. We receive instruction from those who practice it. I shall try to present the study of magic as a special technology, rather than as an arcane mystery available only to a chosen few. There is nothing difficult in the practice of magic. Not everyone is equipped to be a physician, an attorney or an engineer—why should everyone be equipped to be a magician? The talents required are quite different, but the analogy presented is correct. Magic is often presented as a sacred and hidden mystery. Eating our daily bread is a sacred mystery to those of us who have true understanding. There is no more reason to present magic as a mystery than there is to introduce cooking in this way.

If the world had treated electricity with the same awe and superstitious mystery that surrounds the practice of magic, it is unlikely that electrical technology would have progressed to the point where doorbells could exist. It is also highly unlikely that electric lights or telephones would exist! No researcher would be able to successfully push through the veil of mystery that would surround electricity in order to create a useful technology that could be applied by ordinary people.

Throughout this work I have made the point that magic must have a real physical result to be worthy of the name. If an electrician wires a house for electrical illumination, we expect the lights to work. If the lights do not light, the fault is usually with the electrician. If there is no result from an act of magic, the fault is usually with the magician. Results are not too much to expect from our neighborhood magician. Even the learned and licensed professions have a few members who are regarded quietly as frauds by more result-oriented and ethical peers.

Do not expect that everyone who claims to be a magician is one. It is currently popular to define magic as the art of changing our consciousness at will. This is not my definition of magic. Being able to change consciousness at will is a prerequisite to any real practice of magic. The student of magic must gain control of the mind as the first step to learning the art. In the process of gaining control of the mind the magician gains the ability to change the perception of earthly reality at will. In time, as a result of training exercises, the magician gains the ability to enter into any state of consciousness that is available.

Being a magician is a stage in the process of developing spiritually. It is not the height of development; in fact, it is only a step in the first part of the range of real human development. The fact that many religious sects speak and act harshly against those who have the ability to practice magic is most revealing of the true character of the leaders heading these religions. Those whom they speak against may be more developed spiritually than the so-called religious people who speak against them!

Practice
of MAGIC

Chapter 1

THE MODES
OF MAGICAL
PRACTICE

Magic, for the purposes of this work, will be briefly defined as the art of causing observable changes in the physical universe in conformity with the human will. We will later expand on this brief definition, but setting it out here will reveal the basis of our discussion. Anything that might otherwise be considered magic, which is not able to produce a change in the physical universe, will not be a consideration in this work.

There are various modes of magic. These modes are approaches to the practice of magic, not just a set of specific techniques for the performance of any particular magical act. We may consider each of these modes of magic to be classifications of magical philosophy—guides to an understanding of one part of the magical universe. We shall examine the major modes of magic, and attempt to understand how they function to create the change desired in the physical universe when they are applied by their practitioners.

Difficulties present themselves when we examine the subject of magic, not the least of these being our current cultural bend away from the non-physical (or magical) universe toward the material universe. In addition, we are faced with the difficulty that all our various classifications have their origin in the perception of the physical universe as it is reported to us by our sensory organs. Our shared perception of the physical universe by our sensory organs is all that we really have in common with our fellow human beings. Most of us eventually recognize that many of our perceptions, and the experiences resulting from these perceptions, are so unique to us that we cannot really share them with others.

While a majority can agree on observations such as dimension (length, height, breadth), color, and sound, our standards of odor and taste have a great variability, and this makes any observations of these physical senses quite subjective. The more subtle senses—the psychic perceptions—show even greater ranges of variability. Many people seem to be blind, deaf, and dumb to these phenomena, while others have psychic senses as open to these non-physical perceptions as their physical senses are open to physical perceptions.

Both modern and ancient investigations of the manner of perception, and the operation of the human sensory system, reveal that the physical senses and their interpretation are ultimately subjective. They are particular to the individual, rather than objective, and can not always be agreed on by the community. Anthropological research has indicated that physical perception by our sensory organs may be culturally subjective as well, and really not uniform through the human family as a whole. For the majority of humanity, the perceptions of the non-measurable physical, as well as the non-physical senses, are entirely subjective. These perceptions are based upon references which the individual does not share with family or community.

When we classify various modes of magical practice, it will necessarily be subjective and will relate to our individual perceptions. The practice of magic is seldom objective, and is seldom examined objectively by the community. The practice of magic is usually a subjective and personal experience.

Magic will never become a science because it is not measurable, nor can it be precisely replicated. These are the two tests which must be met by any real science. A physician friend said the same thing about the practice of medicine. He told me that while parts of medicine can be very scientific and meet all of the tests of a science, the practice of medicine itself was an art. As with any art, some people are better at performing it than others.

As a practical matter, the mode of magic employed by one person may be entirely unsuitable to another. The mode of magic is not at fault, it is only the unsuitability of that mode for the individual that causes the difficulty.

Bearing in mind our definition of magic as a process that results in real change in the physical world, let us restate it here.

MAGIC – The application of the astral or emotional force of an incarnate human being to the material world, in order to bring about the change in the material world which is desired, as directed by the will power of the incarnate human being.

All magic that results in a perceptible change in the physical universe is the result of the controlled application of parts of the incarnate human being we may refer to as "will power" and as "emotions." The emotional power of an incarnate human being may also be referred to as the astral force, or as astral power. The will power might be referred to as "mental power," but if so, it must be differentiated from rational ability, or the conscious thinking mind.

If we expand this definition to include just how the magical process operates, we will see that the actual process is not different from many other life processes. Magic that produces a result in the physical universe is the consequence of the application of the astral (or emotional) force of an incarnate human being on the conditions of the material world that he or she perceives at the time. This is done in such a way that the material world actually changes in accordance with the will of the person exerting this astral or emotional force. The person applying the astral force is the magician, the physical result of the application of his or her emotional force, directed by the will—is the product of his or her magic.

If we were to describe this as the motion of an arm or a leg, the wording would be the same, because the act of willing the motion of the arm or leg—and the manifestation of the motion in the physical world—is, in fact, carried out through the same process as is the process of magic. In both cases, the will power calls on the astral (or emotional) force to make the change desired. The difference is that in moving the leg, the astral force is applied to a physical part of the person's own body. In magical operations, the astral force is applied to the physical universe—one stage removed from the person.

When there is no physical change in the material world, there is no act of magic. It is the physical change—observable to the point where an impartial observer would agree that a change has occurred—which identifies the magic as real. The ability to consistently obtain such physical changes is what identifies an individual as a magician.

An individual is either a magician or not. This means that someone may study any of the modes of magical practice, but the ability to perform one mode (or many modes) in a consistent manner is what makes a real magician. Reading books doesn't do it. A real magician is neither a deluded fool nor a devotee of weird behavior. A magician is what he or she is, and has no need to convince others of anything. What would we think of physicians or attornies who constantly had to tell others about how powerful they are?

The result of an application of magic is the real physical change in the physical world that the magician *causes*. This change must always be as noticeable to the physical senses of an impartial observer as is the motion of an arm, or the new color of a freshly painted wall. Without this evidence of change there is no magic. The magician must be able to demonstrate this change. It is not enough to feel that the change has, or should have, come about. Without proof that the desired change has occurred, there is no result to the magical attempt, only self-delusion in the mind of the would-be magician.

This is a very important point, although it is conveniently overlooked. Many who consider themselves magicians dwell on ideas of "expanding consciousness," or "joining with the great spiritual forces of the universe," or some such apparently noble cause. Many of these people believe that performing magic which has real results in the physical world is either beneath their power, or a misuse of their ability.

As these would-be magicians do nothing that might disturb the psyche, they can live in a world of fantasy — a world in which they are great magicians! Performing magic with no physical result is just a means of self-delusion. This is not a suitable form of magic for those who sincerely wish to develop themselves. Unfortunately, the fanciful magicians are best known in our society today. Dion Fortune, a well-known magician and occultist, defined magic as "the art of producing changes of consciousness at will." I think that it must be more than that.

Those who find they cannot perform magic with physical results should seek to develop spiritually until they are able to work magic. At a certain point in the development of the human soul, they will be able to perform magic which has a real physical result. This state of being must be reached by everyone seeking to develop harmony with the creator. The ability to perform magic is a spiritual ability, and it must be sought for in the realm of the spirit.

The study of the various modes of magical practice will allow us to see just how it is that the astral force of the magician is directed to operate on the physical world. We will also gain some understanding of the way the mind and emotional nature of the magician must be trained together to make the practice of magic possible. We will learn the similarities and differences between the various modes of magic, and that in many ways, our choice—the mode we individuals use to become magicians—is decided by our culture. We will also learn enough about the various modes of magical practice to understand that the same effect may be obtained in numerous ways, even though individual magicians believe that there is only one way to do something.

Chapter 2

PREPARING TO PRACTICE MAGIC

Despite any of the various accouterments required in the various modes of magical practice, the primary instruments of magicians are their consciousness, their mental faculties, and the physical bodies which house them. To become magical practitioners students must begin training the conscious mental faculties.

Regardless of the particular practice that students intend to master, the first steps on the path are the same. Potential magicians must learn to relax and quiet their physical bodies. Once this is accomplished, they learn to take control of their minds. Until these two steps are mastered there is no sense in going further into the study of any of the various forms of magic. The mastery of these two steps may take willing and enthusiastic students three or four years under the direction of an able teacher. For neophytes working without benefit of the direct instruction of a real teacher, it may take considerably longer.

In our age of "I want this right now," there is a constant search for easy methods and quick solutions. In fact there is no royal road to magical practice, any more than there is a royal road to any other skill or ability. Those who promise quick and easy solutions to complex developmental processes are usually either charlatans, or people who have nothing real to offer students.

Developing yourself for the practice of magic requires a considerable amount of patient effort which is devoted in small bits of time over the course of many years. Eventually the performance of various exercises becomes a habitual part of life. At this point you begin to make progress that gradually becomes apparent.

The first exercise my own teacher gave me was a relaxation exercise. I was given the exercise in the same form that it is given below, and told that I could see him again once I had mastered the exercise by practicing it for at least three months. I returned in four months with the exercise, to my knowledge, completely mastered. My teacher worked with me for about an hour, and showed me that I had only begun to scratch the surface of the exercise. He then sent me away with the admonition to return only when I had mastered the exercise. This time it was six months before I felt that I had some mastery of the exercise and was able to return to him for further guidance. I still practice this relaxation exercise on a daily basis, and intend to do so for the rest of my life.

Relaxation

The tensions of daily life permeate us with their nervous energy. We become unknowing receptors for the thoughts and emotions of others. Until we can learn to relax to a certain depth, and rid ourselves of the tensions of daily life, we are not able to act on the world, much less to discipline our minds. All that we can do in this over-active state is react to influences exerted on us by the world around us.

We can not become ourselves if we are full of muscular and nervous tensions that constantly demand our conscious or subconscious attention. We have nothing within ourselves to develop if we are simply reacting to the influences of the physical and non-physical world around us. In this situation—the situation in which most people live—we are not able to really express our fullest potential.

Human beings were intended by their creator to become forces in the universe. We cannot become active forces in the universe if we are assailed by the universe to the point where we are so fully distracted that we have no time to act on the world in which we live. Relaxation, learning to free ourselves from external tensions, is always the first step in development. Until we can live on Earth in a relaxed and stress-free manner, we are not going to be able to learn how to act on Earth in any real way.

The relaxation exercise is simplicity itself. All that is required is that you relax your physical body as completely as possible for thirty minutes per day. During this time you should learn to ignore any thoughts which may present themselves to your mind. Do not try to blank your mind, just ignore any thoughts which may enter into it. Concentrate your mind only on relaxing your physical body. Relax yourself by releasing all of the tension from your muscles. Simply lay or sit comfortably, and mentally direct your physical body to relax. This is all that there is to it.

Because this exercise is deceptively simple, many people ignore it, to their loss. If you are sincerely interested in improving yourself, to say nothing of learning to practice magic, you will use this exercise to your advantage.

Once you have practiced this exercise for at least six months you should be living your life in a considerably more relaxed state. You will find that this will be of benefit to you in your everyday affairs, as well as giving you some insight into the process of preparing yourself to practice magic.

The next exercise is the one which Aleister Crowley used to develop his magical abilities. Although at the time he received this exercise he was a member of the Order of the Golden Dawn, and considered by most of his associates to be an accomplished magician, he really began developing his magical abilities on a cruise to Mexico. On board the ship he met a man who was also a mountain climber. In conversation they discovered that they were both intending to climb the same mountains in Mexico. In further conversation Crowley revealed his interest in magic to his new acquaintance. The man was not impressed, because he had observed that Crowley was unable to concentrate his mind. He gave Crowley the following exercise, which Crowley mastered on the cruise. Once he had mastered this exercise, he found that his magical abilities improved greatly as a result.

The concentration exercise is given in substantially the same form here as it was given to Aleister Crowley. When you master this exercise you will find that you have gained greater control over your mind.

• Examine any commonplace object: a lead pencil will do. Observe and note as many details as possible in the object. Now set the object aside, and write down as many details as you can recall from memory. Describe the object completely from memory.

• Now reexamine the object, seeking for new details. Put it aside, and once again write down all the new details you discover.

• Lastly, close your eyes, and in a state of relaxation, visualize the object in your mind's eye. See the object in your mind as it is in the physical state, visualizing all of the details you have noted in it. Hold this image as long as you can, adding all of the details you have found in the object.

Practice this exercise with a different familiar object every day for at least three months, while continuing to do your relaxation exercise. This exercise will develop your ability to pay attention. It will also begin developing your ability to observe and concentrate upon objects. You should begin this exercise with simple things, like tableware, pencils, pens and the like. As you perfect yourself with these objects, you may go on to more complex things such as the decor of a room, pictures, etc.

In Rudyard Kipling's book *Kim*, there is a game given to the young boy Kim which is also an exercise in observation. In this game a number of objects are placed on a tray and covered with a cloth. Those who are playing the game are allowed a fixed time to look at the exposed tray, usually a minute for the dozen or so objects which are displayed, and then the cloth is placed over the tray again. With the tray covered, the players write down a list of the objects which they have seen on the tray. The winner is the one who has written down the greatest number of objects on the tray correctly.

While this is an excellent game for pre-teen and teenage children to play at home, it is also an excellent way for adults to develop the powers of observation. While you are doing the relaxation exercises and later when you have added the exercise of studying commonplace objects, you should play this game whenever possible. Play it either with yourself or with others. Simple as it seems, it is an excellent tool for self development.

As I mentioned, these exercises seem to be deceptively simple. However, they have a real, positive, and lasting effect on those who master them. You should take the time to master them if you are serious about striving to develop yourself in any way.

Chapter 3

THE RELIGIOUS RITUAL

O ur study of the modes of magical prac-
tice will begin with the most familiar to us, the magic of
the church service, or religious magic. We will then see
how the ceremonial magic of religious practice came to
become the ritual and ceremonial magic of the magician. Then we shall look at deific magico-religious practices, the religions of pagans in ancient times and of so-
called primitive people today. Finally we shall see the
basis of much of current magical practice in the magic of
the spirits, of the elements, and in natural magic.

Religious ritual is an example of a magical ceremony. This was more true in ancient times than it is
today, but it is still true. In the ancient world, among
our Stone Age ancestors, it was frequently thought that
the ritual observances of the community actually kept
the actions of the seasons on their courses.

Ceremony is a formal act, or a set of acts, conducted in a serious manner, upon an important occasion, for a specific purpose. A ceremony should provide both physical sensory stimulation, and a mental focus upon the intention of the ceremony. A well-performed ceremony will draw the focus of attention of both observers and participants. The ceremony will capture their attention, while it also stimulates the emotions.

Religious ceremony, especially in the established churches, has this quality. No one who has viewed a pontifical high mass could fail to be impressed by the ritual observances, from the sound of the choir to the visual richness of the worship. The English Coronation Ceremony, the Inauguration of the President of the United States, are all major ceremonies of great effect.

We might say that these ceremonies also fulfill our requirements for magic, but some of them do so in an entirely intellectual way. The person inaugurated President is now allowed to be the President, but that person has not undergone any perceptible physical change as a result of the ceremony of inauguration. The same is true of a religious ceremony. There is no perceptible physical change in the worshiper as a result of attending a religious ceremony. Effective religious ceremony does, however, cause a definite temporary emotional change in the worshiper.

This emotional change is the desired end of most religious ceremonies. Emotional change in the worshiper is the desired goal of every Protestant Christian revival service. Even the best Protestant revival speakers are aware that the congregation's emotional change is usually for the short term, lasting at best a few days. The emotional effect of the revival ceremony provides the worshiper with an emotional catharsis, and this is the main feature of Protestant fundamentalist religious practice in the United States.

Ritual is the repetitive performance of a set form of ceremony. Ritual involves at least an action, usually accompanied by spoken words, on the part of the person performing it. The action and spoken words, and other additions used to enhance the value of the ceremony, must be repeated frequently, over a period of time, to become a ritual.

Religious ritual, unchanging over a long period of time, develops another quality. The emotional force (astral force) generated in the worshipers through the constant repetition of religious rites, attains a life of its own in what are referred to as thought forms. These thought forms are containers of the emotional (or the astral) energy generated by the worshipers. They are fed and are re-enforced by the emotional (astral) energy of worship. The emotional energy of the worshipers naturally builds the astral thought form.

Thought forms are blind forces; they have no reasoning ability and no selectivity. In a number of respects, the emotional nature may be compared to water. If you place your hand into water, your hand will get wet. If you enter into a thought form, you will respond to the emotional energy stored within it. The degree of response you will have to any particular thought form will be in direct proportion to the amount of the same kind of emotional (astral) energy within you. If you are "religious" in a particular religion, and you enter a place where there is a large thought form of that religion present, it will cause a stronger response on your part than it would for a "non-religious" person.

Entering into the thought form of a religion will cause some emotional response in everyone, although the individual may not be conscious of it. Almost everyone has some conception of religion, usually learned in childhood, that is part of his or her emotional makeup.

It is the emotional (astral) thought form that gives certain churches and holy sites an aura or feeling of sanctity. This aura or thought form stimulates an emotion, interpreted as a feeling of spirituality, in those who enter the church or holy site. A thought form which has been developed over a long period of time, through frequent repetition of the same religious ceremonies, will enforce a subconscious belief in the precepts of the religion upon those who enter into or worship within the church.

The strength of thought forms is directly proportional to the emotional (astral) energy within them. This energy is directly dependent upon the emotional (astral) energy available to those worshipers who are believers in the religious practice. It is the emotional energy of the believing worshiper, radiated during the worship service, which forms and feeds the thought form. Further, worshipers are stimulated to release and radiate emotional (astral) energy by the presence of the thought form itself.

One of the original purposes of the ceremony of consecration of a Roman Catholic Church, or an earlier pagan temple, was to install a thought form into the building, although this is not a reason given in the modern Roman Ritual. The installation of this thought form will occur if those who participate in the consecration are believers in the religion, and radiate sufficient emotional energy during the ceremony of consecration.

When we enter a church, cathedral, or temple containing a strong thought form, it is both easy and common to interpret the emotional impact of the thought form as a spiritual experience. It is not possible for most of us to differentiate between an emotional and a spiritual experience. The presence of the constantly renewed thought form, in itself, can enforce the belief of the emotional (astral) part of the worshiper in the theological views presented by the religion. This encourages the worshiper to release even more emotional energy to the thought form in the act of worship.

One of the reasons that the conservative Catholic Latin Mass is so effective is that the Trinitarian Latin Mass has been in daily use throughout the world for over five hundred years. It has a fully developed ritual thought form, one of the most powerful in the world. At one time every Roman Catholic priest in the world said the Latin Mass every day, in the same way. As this was done in the same language, all over the world, tremendous emotional energy was placed into the thought form. The energy of this thought form was huge in its extent. Despite its lesser intensity today, having been replaced in the Roman Catholic Church by the vernacular mass, the older Latin Mass thought form is still powerful, a thought form which will take at least a century or more to dissipate.

The change from the Latin Mass to the vernacular mass caused many Catholics to remark that "something was missing" in their worship. What was missing was the power of the thought form of the Latin Mass. It will take hundreds of years for the vernacular mass to build a thought form as the Latin Mass did. Even then, the thought form of the vernacular mass will be limited in extent to those nations where the mass is said in the same way and in the same language. Meanwhile the Latin Mass will still continue to have a stronger emotional impact on the believing Roman Catholic than the vernacular mass.

One of the reasons for the surge of growth of Islam in the world today is the force of the thought form generated by the prayers repeated five times a day by the devote Muslims of the world. The force of this religious thought form exerts a real emotional pressure on the faithful, and on others whom they contact. The prayers of the pious in any religion both strengthen the faith of all those who practice the religion, and fabricate a thought form blanket which covers the members of the religious sect with a feeling of emotional comfort and security. This is one of the reasons why religion, when practiced piously, is such an emotional comfort to the believer.

The subconscious mind is both illogical and unquestioning. It will accept anything presented to it as a truth, particularly when it is presented by someone whom the subconscious mind considers an authority. When the acceptance of the subconscious mind is matched by the astral authority of a strong and energetic thought form, the "truth" of the religion is completely accepted by the individual at the emotional (astral) level of being. The individual has actually accepted a set of belief structures. These beliefs are "true" in the religion and in the culture in which they are accepted. It would be highly unlikely that they were actually truths of God from on high, as each religion has its own idea of what these truths are. It is difficult to view God, the Creator and Sustainer of the universe, as one who is undecided about what is true from his perspective.

When there is discord between the observed facts of the universe, as presented through the physical senses to the believing individual, and the belief structures that have been accepted by the subconscious mind, there is a separation which occurs in the mentation (thinking-rational) process. If an individual is forced to accept observed facts of the physical world, and to live within that reality, any religion that teaches an opposite or conflicting worldview usually loses credence in the mind of that individual. It is mental stress over this point—the conflict between religious teaching and the individual's observed facts of life on Earth—which causes "loss of faith," or at least the weakening of faith, over the course of a lifetime.

This clash can be seen in the success of missionary efforts in primitive cultures. The missionaries are usually supported by physical amenities which are indicative of great wealth to the primitive culture. Yet the religion of the primitive culture has told its believers that it has supplied all sorts of physical wealth to those who are its believers. The dichotomy usually results in members of the primitive culture converting to the new religion, to gain the economic benefit that they observe the new God can provide.

In settled religious cultures, the mental stress in the individual is frequently over whatever is repressed by established religion. Sexual repression leads to people breaking away from their religion for sexual relief, which their separation from the religion will, at least in part, allow. This is one of the causes of "loss of faith" in the Romance Language cultures of Europe, as well as the classic reason usually given for the separation from Rome of the Church of England.

Separation from our original childhood belief structure is an important point. It does not matter whether it is an accepted belief structure of a religious or secular nature. The mental act of separation from the childhood belief structure always places a strain upon our mental processes. In many cases severe separation from an accepted belief structure, resulting in emotional trauma, can be a causative factor of demonstrated mental pathologies.

In times of stress and emotional trauma, deep-seated religious beliefs come to the fore. As we pass into old age and move toward death, the religious beliefs of childhood begin to present themselves again in daily life. At times of emotional trauma, the fundamental religious beliefs of childhood overcome any intellectually acquired rationality, or any other belief to which we have made an intellectual or superficial emotional conversion. The ultimate cause of this reversal of belief is the discipline enforced on minds of believers by the thought forms of the religion of the childhood. The "truth" of these beliefs, having been demonstrated to our subconscious minds in earliest childhood will usually surface to overcome any later creations of belief which have only intellectual authority (or a lighter emotional acceptance) to demonstrate their validity.

It is emotion and the repetition of ceremony that builds thought forms, and thus develops any ritual. Variations of ceremony, such as language, ritual action, order of service, all have tendencies to form new thought forms. These new thought forms are weak, they do not have the effect of the well-established thought forms built by the continuous ritual use of the same ceremony.

Should you become a priest, priestess, or other practitioner of a religious ritual, the truth of the religion, which has become a basic truth of your life, is re-enforced by your acceptance of your role as a "priest" of the religious practice. Through this acceptance of both the religious ritual and place in the religious system, you are then able to manifest works of "magic," dependent upon the ability of your astral nature to do so. The other caveat is the tenets of the religion allowing such works to manifest. Many religions foolishly deny the possibility of magic to their priesthoods.

It is through this process that priests or priestesses, as believing members of a particular religious practice, are able to manifest what are called "miracles" during their lifetimes. The late Padre Pio of the Roman Catholic Church is an excellent example of this. The ability of priests to perform valid exorcisms and healings are other less spectacular examples. It is the people who are able to perform miracles that testify to the validity of any religion, for any religion is always built upon its living saints, not its outward earthly hierarchy.

The manner in which the deceased "saints" of a religion are able to manifest miracles, when appealed to in prayer after their death, is similar to the process by which a priest or a living saint can manifest miracles when alive. In the case of most of the deceased "saints," the miracle depends more on the astral force of the living human being who is praying than it does upon the astral force of the "saint." Some of the "saints" of various religions have large thought forms acquired by the veneration of their cultus. The astral force of the thought form of these saints can assist in bringing about the desired miracle.

Religious magic is rare in the better known "main line" religions in the United States today. In the Middle Ages, religious magic was more common. At one time it was believed that people could actually be killed by having a priest say a funeral mass for them while the person was still alive. Masses are frequently said for an intention, a purpose of some kind, and usually the intention is for the repose of the soul of departed members of the congregation.

The central prayer of the weekday Jewish services, the Amidah, contains thirteen sections of requests, including a final section in which the worshiper may add requests to meet his or her own needs. Many of the standard prayerbooks suggest either a prayer for forgiveness or a prayer for prosperity at this point. The standard Hebrew prayer books have prayers for almost every occasion, including prayers for good weather and many other human intentions. This procedure of having a variety of prayers for different intentions is also followed by the Episcopal church in the United States. Other Protestant denominations seem to feel that any prayer for material goals is the work of the devil. By having a theology that denies the possibility of religious magic, the religion makes it impossible for their clergy to ever perform it.

There are now a number of lesser known religions in the United States and these groups practice magic as a part of their regular religious practice. Many of these are pagan and neo-pagan religions that seemed to come out of the 1960s. Other magical religions found in the larger cities are Afro-American religions. It is likely that within a few generations these religions will have developed a clergy that will be adept at religious magic. This ability has already been demonstrated in the Christian Science religion, where each successive generation of "readers" generally has greater ability to heal the sick who come to them.

A striking example of religious magic is the act of infant Baptism, found in the Christian religion. This act is a real religious ritual, although it is often felt to be only a socially useful device in the majority of main line protestant churches. Yet, in the Roman Catholic Church, it has a much greater significance. If conducted according to the complete Roman Ritual, it first is an exorcism of all evil influences from the infant, the infant's first spiritual cleansing. Secondly, the ritual opens the path for the infant to become a member of the family of the body of Christ, by sealing the infant to Christ, through the consecrated water of the ritual of baptism. Thirdly, it attempts to insure the participation of the infant in the community of Christian believers by providing a set of God parents, who are to stand for the child in addition to the natural parents, to insure that the child is brought up to become a full member of the Christian religion. If the ritual of Baptism is understood in this way, it can be recognized as a powerful religious ritual which may have a lasting effect in the life of the child.

The Roman church is not the only Christian religion which treats Baptism with this degree of seriousness. Some of the more fundamentalist protestant denominations do as well. Whenever a child is baptized by a priest or pastor who treats the act with the consideration it deserves, the child will become more likely to follow the religion in their later years. The strong thought form of the religion being impressed on them in a solemn ceremony of religious magic at an early age, it is much more likely that the infant will continue as a believer in the religion as they grow older.

As an example of a religious ritual which does not conflict with any religious creed, and which usually has beneficial results for the person who regularly performs it, the following prayer to the guardian angel may be used on a Monday morning before starting off for work.

Take a small white candle, a birthday candle will do, and light it while saying the following prayer to your guardian angel.

You who are with me in this life as my guide and protector, I express my gratitude to you with this candle which I light for you. I thank you for your loving care and guidance.

Allow the candle to burn out.

As Christian, Jewish and Islamic religious practices all have at least some belief in a guardian angel, this prayer does not conflict with any of them. In addition, it seems to have had good results for those who have used it for at least six months.

Chapter 4

RITUAL AND CEREMONIAL MAGIC

Ritual and Ceremonial Magic is what is most commonly called "magic" in the Western world. In the early middle ages the practice of Ritual and Ceremonial Magic was regarded as an art similar to philosophy. It was thought to be a valid means of dealing directly with the invisible higher forces of the universe. Educated gentlemen were expected to have some understanding of the art of Ritual and Ceremonial Magic, just as they were expected to have some understanding of philosophy.

Ritual and Ceremonial Magic in Europe, from the time of the Roman Empire to the Reformation, was completely intertwined with the prevailing religion of the times. As Christianity came to power with Constantine, magic quickly became Christian in nature. Many well-worn magical ceremonies, some so old that they come from the Babylonian era, assumed the new theological garb of the Christian Religion.

Christian religious practices imposed on the ancient Babylonian magic circle the names of the four Jewish angels of the quarters. It also replaced the names of the deities of the Babylonian Pantheon with the names of the Roman Pantheon for the planetary forces, and the names of the Hebrew deity of the Old Testament for the names of the attributes of the Creator-Godhead.

Christian theology added another force to be reckoned with in magic. The Devil, who was considered only a minor annoyance in Judaism and Babylonia, became the direct opponent of God in the Christian worldview. While this concept followed the Persian Zoroastrian world view of a constant duel between the forces of good and evil, it was foreign to the Jewish tradition and ancient Babylonian and Sumerian belief and practices. Christian magicians who failed in their art now had the Devil, and the loss of their souls to Hell to fear, according to the theologians.

Failure in Christian magic had such a high price that it was generally considered better to think about magic than it was to perform it. The medieval philosophers did a lot of thinking and writing about magic, but they did very little actual magical work. We shall see that this intellectual attitude concerning practical magic continues to the present day.

Ritual and Ceremonial Magic is usually considered to be "high magic" in contrast to the "low magic" of deific magic, witchcraft, or necromancy. The practice of high magic required at least the ability to read and write, something which "low magic" did not require. High magic contrasted quite vividly with the simpler practice of Witchcraft. Witchcraft was the province of illiterate country folk, while high magic was the province of townspeople, and more especially, the well-educated clerics and nobility.

There is one other major contrast between the "high magic" of the educated classes and the "low magic" of the countryside. Low magic usually worked for the performer, producing results in the physical world. The more elaborate and theoretically theologically sound "high magic" usually did not produce any physical results. High magic did work well enough to keep its reputation for danger, but it did not work for all those who tried it. Results of any kind, in the practice of high magic, were always sporadic; and they always depended upon the individual magician. We will now examine the more formal high magic of ceremony and ritual as it is practiced today.

I explained earlier that all religious services are ceremony. Some religions make their services more of a ritual ceremony than others. A few religions have the hour for attendance at the service as their only point of ritual. The ritual of any religion is the basis for the construction of a thought form that envelopes worshipers in a shared emotional experience of the religion, and which emotionally energizes worshipers in their worship of God.

Ritual magic was the basis of most of the ancient mystery religions. In the sense that we have discussed it to this point, we could say that it is still the basis of most of the world's religions. Religion is, to a large extent, a practice of ritual and ceremonial magic. Like many practices of ritual magic, it desires to have a result in the non-physical world, rather than a result in the physical world. In fact, the result is always emotional in nature.

In religion, or in ritual magic, there is always a certain amount of emotional energy released in the ceremony. It is the release of this emotional energy which can act to make a change in the emotional nature of the person who is involved in either magic or religion. It is this release of emotional energy which is usually understood to be the change of consciousness, the goal sought by the majority of practitioners of ritual magic. This same release of emotional energy could also be applied to make real changes in the physical world.

Ritual magic need not deal either with a deity or with a pantheon of deities. When ritual magic is oriented to a particular pantheon, it quickly becomes a magico-religious practice. The ceremonies of ritual magic may or may not make use of so-called Extra Human Intelligences, spirits, elementals, angels or demons. Much time and effort of the more scholarly adherents of ritual magic in the middle ages was spent in developing long lists of these spirits and demons, along with the theoretical means of summoning them up to do the will of the magician. These scholarly magical philosophers produced few real results in the magical work they actually performed.

Ritual magic, with all the frills removed, is simply the use of ceremony or ritual. This ceremony or ritual can be whatever is required to make the magic produce the results desired on the physical plane. The fact that a particular ceremony or ritual dates from antiquity is no guarantee that it is either better or worse than a ceremony or ritual which is made up by the magician on the spur of the moment.

Benvenuto Cellini, the famous goldsmith and artist, reported in his autobiography a rather emotional result to a complex magical evocation in the Roman Forum.

Like many people who have experimented from casual curiosity with ritual and ceremonial magic, Cellini witnessed some results from the evocation of spirits. The forms and shapes he was able to view in the Forum frightened him, apparently so badly that he never repeated the experiment. Lee R. Gandee reported the excellent results he had in assisting some distressed people with an incantation using the Latin botanical names of trees in his book *Strange Experiences*.[1] His remarks, in the chapter titled "Go Fetch My Thighbone" illustrates graphically that magic is a belief structure which operates when the subconscious mind is impressed with the force of a suggestion that the magic will be effective. This suggestion is powered by the emotional (or astral) force of the thought forms of those who participate in the ritual. It is suggestion, and the resultant emotional force of those who participate in the ritual that makes the ritual have the results it may be able to manifest in the physical world.

The ceremonies of ritual and ceremonial magic are usually rigidly structured, more so in some magical systems than in others. These ceremonies are usually intended to have only one purpose, so a new ceremony must be constructed for each purpose desired. True practitioners of this magical art usually have a vast repertory of ceremonies to draw from. The nature of rituals currently in print range over every conceivable form of human desire. Some of the rituals are really silly and have been republished in the last few years.

---

[1]Lee R. Gandee, *Strange Experiences* (Englewood Cliffs, NJ: Prentice Hall, 1971) pp. 332–336.

A few of the better books concerning the fundamentals of ritual and ceremonial magic include basic rituals that can be altered to allow the operator to direct the ritual to whatever end he or she desires. This is a considerably more sound practice, magically, as the thought form of the basic ritual is built, and reinforced, with each repetition of the basic ritual. Thus, the thought form of the basic ritual will keep growing from the emotional energy of the practitioner and whomever assists the practitioner in the work. David Conway's book, *Magic: An Occult Primer,* is an excellent example of this kind of book. Mr. Conway gives two different types of rituals that suit most human needs.[2]

Ceremonies and rituals of this type of magic are longer and much more involved than the shorter spells of countryfolk. Short spells, often rhymed, are favored by those who use natural magic in their work. Complex rituals seem to make a deep impression on the impressionable subconscious mind. With natural magic, the impression is not transferred through suggestion. The impression is imposed upon the receiving mind, which unhesitatingly accepts it as a command.

The rituals of Ritual and Ceremonial Magic are expensive, and take time and equipment to complete. In addition, they require study and leisure, luxuries which are seldom available to the poor. Ritual and Ceremonial Magic requires the use of a number of what a stranger would probably refer to as theatrical props. There are special swords, censers, vestments, and other implements. Different implements may be required for each ceremony being performed. The grimories of the

---

[2]See David Conway, *Magic: An Occult Primer* (New York: E. P. Dutton, 1972).

middle ages listed many of these accessory items in great detail.

Special ceremonies in the practice of ritual and ceremonial magic may require an unusual location, a temple of a certain shape, a mountain top, a graveyard, or the like. With all of the theatrics required, Ritual and Ceremonial Magic makes a stimulating subject for stories. It provides a dramatic performance, so it is quite reasonable to see it stressed as "magic" in the popular novels.

Peter Carroll has explained the necessity of these theatrical effects in the following way in his excellent book for the more advanced magician.

> Much of the paraphernalia and theory of magic, including this theory, exist partly to convince the magician that he is a magician and magic is possible in a cultural climate which is heavy (heavily) antagonistic to such notions.[3]

Because Ritual and Ceremonial Magic is suited for group as well as individual use, it forms the basis for the many "Occult Lodges" found in fictional accounts of the occult. Tales of groups of evil magicians titillate readers of such literature, and there is certainly enough ritual material in print to allow authors to situate their novels accurately. Unfortunately most stories are only remotely based on fact. True stories of magical practice would either be unbelievable or boring to the average reader. True magical lodges are no more thrilling to participate in than assemblages of old men at a pensioners

---

[3]Peter J. Carroll, *Liber Kaos* (York Beach, ME: Samuel Weiser, 1992), p. 30.

club who gather to play cards. Lodges of the kind illustrated in fiction no longer exist today, if they ever did.

The kind of magic which most current Ritual and Ceremonial Magicians practice can be found in their published magical records. One such example is found in *Dancers to the Gods* edited by Alan Richardson.[4] Results similar to those obtained by these magicians could also be obtained with any of the hallucinogenic drugs available today. These results can also be obtained by anyone who wishes to engage in a group mental fantasy. I do not consider these effects to be magic, as there is no physical result.

As an example of magic with a physical result, worked by a magician in the same, or at least quite similar, ceremonial magic system:

> . . . dead sparrows started turning up in our yard. Some mornings, several at a time. . . . Robby conjured up the Mars Sphere aspect of Baal, and put him on guard, patrolling our property. The instances of the dead birds stopped as suddenly as it started, and a few days later one of our neighbors moved out in the middle of the night.[5]

While so-called "Occult Lodges" that practice Ritual and Ceremonial Magic are to be found in every major city, they are usually much more pretense than reality. They

---

[4]Alan Richardson, Ed., *Dancers to the Gods* (London: Aquarian Press, 1985).
[5]Paraphrased from *Secret Lodge* (Cincinnati, OH: Black Moon Publishing Co., 1984), Archives, FA#1 p. 6.

afford an outlet for the dramatic abilities of some individuals. They are neither evil, nor spiritual. They are also not long-lasting nor of any particular benefit to their members. Serious students of Ceremonial Magic usually avoid them.

Training to become a ritual or ceremonial magician is a long and difficult process. It requires the acceptance of a set of beliefs that are able to override the usual cultural inhibitions to the working of magic. The mental structures within the mind of the magician must be accepted with enough enthusiasm to allow them to be released with full emotional power during the ritual. The subconscious force of the operator must be applied in the direction of the will of the magician for the magic to be successful. This force must be able to bypass any subconscious inhibitions to applying the full astral force of the operator to the work at hand.

As with any magical practice, the consciousness of the operator must be in agreement with the goal at hand. Both conscious and subconscious minds must be focused toward the chosen goal. Only in this way can the full astral force of the magician be brought to bear on the ritual.

Considering that most people cannot keep attention focused on any goal for more than a few minutes, this is a very difficult thing, indeed. It is to this goal that the magician-in-training first directs attention. One popular training manual has as its first exercise: "Observe your train of thought without the slightest digression for a time of at least 10 minutes."[6]

---

[6]F. Bardon, *Initiation into Hermetics* (Wuppertal, Germany: Ruggeberg Verlag, 1962), p. 52.

As with most of the exercises of Ritual and Ceremonial Magic, there are benefits to be obtained from the exercise, regardless of whether or not students are able to master the magical art itself. The benefits to be gained from following a serious course of study are one of the main attractions for serious neophytes. Those who become real magicians are often considered to be changed people, in that they are able to interrelate with the world in a more positive manner as a result of their mental training.

Psychologists realize that inhibitions, fears, and guilts are the major barriers between the individual and his or her true self. For the most part, these negative emotions are learned through social conditioning, which begins impinging upon the individual at birth, and which does not cease until death. The individual who wishes to perform magic must clear away these barriers of conditioned emotion. Most of the training in magical practice is initially directed to this end. Obviously, most people never manage to clear away these emotional barriers at all.

Developing control of the mind and the emotions is a goal for many people, as is ridding oneself of their inhibitions, fears and guilts. That this can be accomplished through the sort of training which a ceremonial magician undergoes is one of the reasons why some people, who have no initial interest in magic, undergo the long and difficult training. It is a selling point of the system, so to speak.

The process of removing the barriers between the apparent self and the true self is the beginning of the mastery of magic—not the end. This is the state of becoming a clear vessel or a "blank slate." Attaining this goal is one of the reasons why the better known systems of ceremonial magic, particularly those derived from the works of Aleister Crowley, make the "Knowledge and Conversation of the Holy Guardian Angel" one of the most important tasks of the ceremonial magician. Crowley used as his grimoire *The Book of the Sacred Magic of Abra-Melin, the Mage*, but it is still debated by his followers whether or not he actually completed the work.[7] Many of those who have attempted to follow in his footsteps in this work have reported a variety of strange experiences using this grimoire. It is even claimed that some have lost their minds through working with it. It is not a system of magic to be recommended.

Only when this conversation has been achieved, usually through other practices, and the "true will" of the magician realized, is it possible for magicians to use ritual and ceremony to obtain whatever they desire. Desires are always in accord with the true will however, and it is necessary to note that it might be the true will of the magician to be something other than a magician. In this case, the people who have come this far along the path at least realize what their true will actually is!

Group magical work is much the same. The ability of a group to perform magic is limited by the various fears, guilts, and inhibitions of the members of the group. As a result, there is little real work accomplished by most groups. The old adage that a camel is an animal designed by a committee applies to magical groups as well. Most of the modern magical groups I have seen would be lucky to come up with a camel.

-----

[7]This 15th-century grimoire was translated and edited by S. L. MacGregor-Mathers (New York: Causeway Books, 1974).

A friend once commented that a certain magical group was quite successful in their magical work. He added that when this group entered a room it had the same effect as an Army Special Forces A Team entering a room. Not only were all eyes drawn to them, because of the power they exuded, but their very presence and vitality changed the atmosphere of the room.

It requires the same kind of careful selection of personnel, dedicated work, and discipline to form an active magical group as it does to form an Army Special Forces A Team. Most occult groups do not have a chance of attaining that level of ability. All the members of the lodge must willingly submit themselves to develop discipline and harmony before such an effect can be realized. Most groups usually spend their time socializing and engaging in mutual self-delusion. This was actually the end goal of the most famous magical order of the English speaking world, the hermetic Order of the Golden Dawn. Ellic Howe has treated this sorry story in his book *The Magicians of the Golden Dawn*.[8]

Because of the difficulty of having a group able to actually manifest anything in the physical world, the application of Ritual and Ceremonial Magic in modern times has been to "expand the consciousness" of the magician. The aim of allowing the magician to work up to the ultimate, as the knowledge and conversation of his Holy Guardian Angel, has made magic a form of psychological self-development. The benefit of this is psychological stability, which allows the magician to

---

[8]Ellic Howe, *The Magicians of the Golden Dawn* (York Beach, ME: Samuel Weiser, and London: Aquarian Press, 1978). The book is now out of print.

gain a better material life while presumably developing spiritually.

In ancient times the path of development had a different aim. Ritual and Ceremonial Magic were used to arrive at more worldly goals. The use of ritual and ceremony was a technique, while spiritual development, which allowed the individual to use the technique effectively, was reached by a path no longer a part of the modern body of magical knowledge. This path involved the guidance of a spiritual teacher.

The rites of Ritual and Ceremonial Magic provide physical sensory stimulation to assist the mental focus on the intent of the ceremony. The senses must be stimulated to aid the magician in maintaining the mental focus required. Colors, odors, patterns, sounds, and tactile impressions should all contribute harmoniously to the ceremony. Harmony is accomplished by connecting the intentions of the ritual and the sensory stimulants through a system of correspondences. These correspondences are connections, either theoretical or real, between the physical realm and the astral realm. The belief in correspondences is derived from the concept that every astral influence manifests in some way in the physical realm. This is expressed by the well-known Emerald Tablet statement of antiquity, "As above, so below."[9]

The particular system of correspondences used depends upon the system of ritual and ceremonial magic being used. The system of correspondences used depends on the cultural and social biases of the particu-

---

[9]A discussion of the Emerald Tablet may be found in the Appendix, on page 151.

lar magical system. Magicians either make these connections for themselves, or more frequently, they learn them from books or teachers. Making the connections yourself, while much more difficult, is more reliable.

To perform Ritual and Ceremonial Magic with facility, it is necessary that the subconscious mind accept as a matter of absolute truth a particular set of correspondences. The set of correspondences accepted is always a powerful belief structure, which may or may not actually conform to the divine reality. Whether it is an accurate map of the astral universe or not, the set of correspondences must be made a part of the deeply accepted beliefs of the person, and must be wholly integrated within the consciousness.

For the practitioner of Ritual or Ceremonial Magic, the acceptance of this belief structure is not negative. It is necessary that the practitioner never be placed into circumstances which might cause the roots of this belief structure to be shaken. This is one reason why rituals that have no physical result are much safer for the magician. A real crack in the belief structure, such as finding that productions are of no value in the material world, could result in damage to the process of mentation. The rational thinking mind, and the ability to exert the will of the magician would both be damaged. At the very least this would make the magician unsuitable for the further practice of his magical art. In the case of those who lack mental stability, it could cause complete mental breakdown, even insanity. This is one of the much touted "dangers" of working with ritual and ceremonial magic, although it is one of very rare occurrence.

The most widely adopted set of belief structures in the present field of ceremonial magic is based upon the Hebrew Qabbalah. Its symbol, known as the Tree of Life, is based upon ten emanations or spheres, and a pattern of interconnecting paths between them. All of the various facets of the physical world are located, by correspondence, on this Tree of Life. Some facets are found on a sphere, while others are found on one of the interconnecting paths between two spheres. The system is quite complex, and has intellectually challenged some of the greatest minds the human race has produced.

The difficulty with this particular set of beliefs is that it is more limited than one would imagine. While it is certainly an elegant and very wordy system, admirably suited to the presentation of Jewish religious mysticism in its original incarnation, it is not a complete magical system at all, and was never intended to be. In the predecessor to the Jewish system there were only eight spheres, with optionally added interconnecting paths. These eight were expanded to ten spheres to suit the requirements of Jewish religious practice, in which a minion of ten men is required to offer prayers to God. Through this expansion, the original eight spheres lost their original meaning and much of their real value for most practical magical work.

On the other hand, the Qabbalah is an excellent magical system for those who are practitioners of the Jewish religion, especially those who are members of the strictly orthodox Hasidic branch of Judaism. This still means that it is useless, or nearly so, for those who are neither orthodox Jews, or at the very least, literate in Hebrew. Cabalism quickly becomes an exercise in futility for most of the modern followers of ceremonial magic, who have "christianized" it, however mentally pleasing it may be.

As with any magical system, there is a minimum which can be accomplished with it. But it must be noted that placing the system in your subconscious mind means that you can never go beyond the minimum. When you desire to use the Qabbalah for magic, you will place a close limit on yourself.[10]

Aside from the various ritual and ceremonial magical systems which are in use today, there are also a number of other systems which could be developed to at least the extent of the Qabbalah, and some to an even deeper extent. Those who are believing Roman Catholics could use the meditations of St. Ignatius Loyola, the founder of the Society of Jesus. These exercises can develop the spiritual faculties, and through them, an excellent set of worldly correspondences can be fit into the Stations of the Cross. This would better fit into the Christian world view, and allow a much greater facility with Ritual and Ceremonial Magic than the Qabbalah ever can for believing Christians. The fourteen stations of the cross can also be fit into the minor arcana of the tarot very well, each station matching one card in each of the four suits. Each of the tarot suits has an elemental attribution, thus each of the stations of the cross could be viewed from the point of each of the four elements. The meditations could then be fit into the major arcana of the tarot, as further steps or events in the life of Christ, or attributes of Christ as the redeemer of humanity.

The tarot trumps, or major arcana, are enthusiastically fitted into the Qabalistic tree by those who call

---

[10]Incidentally, the word *Qabbalah* is used to indicate the Christianized system used for magic, while *Kaballah* refers to the orthodox Jewish meditative mystical system, according to current Jewish Kabalistic usage.

themselves Christian Qabalists, along with everything else in the known universe. The tarot cards, themselves, can be developed as a separate system of belief, and used as the foundation of a system of ritual and ceremonial magic on their own. This may be done without consideration of any theoretical connection to the Qabbalah they may have accumulated. Having twenty-two places to classify things is not necessarily a virtue. Using the tarot trumps and the minor arcana for ritual work, within their own context of belief, would bring them a little closer to their original intention, but not much. The tarot trumps are not a part of the Hebrew Qabbalah, and never have been. They were placed there by enthusiastic amateurs who noticed a correspondence between the twenty-two letters of the Hebrew alphabet, the twenty-two major trumps, and the twenty-two spheres and paths of the Qabbalah. The correspondence is false, no matter how widely it is believed in.

Another ceremonial magical system in use today is the system of Enochian Magic attributed to Dr. John Dee. The complete system was revealed to him through the agency of spirits speaking through the medium Edward Kelley in the late 1500s. Today we would say that it was a channeled system of magic. The original papers referring to this work were lost, shortly after the death of Dr. Dee. Eventually they were partly recovered, and ultimately donated to the British Museum, where they are today. In their journey, many of the pages of Dr. Dee's original papers met their fate by being used to start kitchen cooking fires by the hand of a maidservant who probably had no interest at all in magic. Regardless of what one thinks of this elaborate system of magic, it is an incomplete system. Those

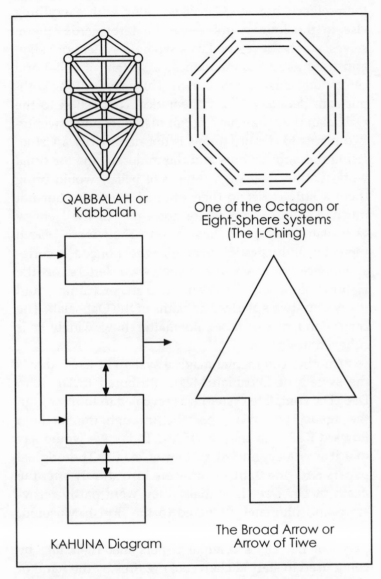

QABBALAH or
Kabbalah

One of the Octagon or
Eight-Sphere Systems
(The I-Ching)

KAHUNA Diagram

The Broad Arrow or
Arrow of Tiwe

Figure 1. Various diagrams of the human being and
the universe. All are equally valid, depending on your
point of view.

destroyed pages cannot be replaced. Incomplete as it is, the system has attracted the attention of a number of enthusiastic adherents, most of whom have qabbalized it, by applying it to the Hebrew system which originally had no contact with it at all.

Enochian magic is well enough loved as a magical system to have its own computer programs, graph paper and numerous textbooks. Many people who have used it say that it is very practical and useful, in the sense of being useful in obtaining physical results. Others have said that it is useful for changing their consciousness. It is definitely one of the more popular systems of Ceremonial Magic.

The point I am attempting to make is that there is no one rigidly held system of magical beliefs that must be adhered to at all costs. A useful Ritual and Ceremonial Magical system can be constructed out of whatever imagery and devices the individual desires. All that is required is that the system allow the rational and emotional minds to harmonize themselves to operate together. Unfortunately, many of those who decide to practice ritual and ceremonial magic find that forcing the more popular "Christian" Qabbalistic system into their subconscious minds is the most available means of learning the techniques.

The original system using eight spheres, the very ancient predecessor to the Jewish Kabbalah, is still available to those who have to learn how to use it. The system has occasionally been written about in the last decade, but I have never seen a book devoted to it in any detail, and do not expect to. The system is known as "The Eight" among those who use it. The I Ching is one of its effects, which may be used for divination, but the I Ching is not a base for the system.

Ritual and Ceremonial Magic may also be used by those who have no knowledge of anything but the basic ritual at hand. If someone knows a ritual, and has full faith and belief in its efficacy, it is quite possible to "work magic" with it. In this case the ritual is its own belief structure. The ritual works because both the subconscious and conscious mind of the operator are in full agreement that it works. There are no fears, guilts, or inhibitions that stand in the way of the performance of the ritual. This results in the full astral power of the magician being employed in the manifestation of the physical change desired by the operator.

Rituals designed only to fulfill the wishes of the operator are of this nature. In this case, the individual believes in the ritual without reservation, with the full intensity of his or her emotions. Once the ritual is carried out, the result is assured, so far as it is possible for the astral nature of the operator to make the results desired manifest.

An example of this type of ritual and ceremonial magic is the "Cup Wish" ritual, which is still practiced among some people in southern West Virginia. The first requirement is a cup, usually an ordinary coffee or tea cup. The person who is to use the spell must personally purchase this cup, so that there is no doubt as to who owns it. The second requirement is that this cup be "Fixed" for the person who is to use it by a locally recognized "person of power." The person of power is usually someone who is considered to be either a witch or a magician in the community. There is usually some difficulty attached to getting the cup fixed, because the magician who is to fix the cup must require the receiver of the cup to do something. Once the cup is "fixed," the person making the wish is given the details of the spell that makes the spell work. The receiver of the cup now sets the cup aside, not using it except when working the spell.

In the future, all the owner of the cup has to do to obtain what he or she desires is to perform the spell exactly as instructed. Often this involves sitting with the cup at the kitchen table, writing out briefly whatever is desired, and burning the paper in the cup. Occasionally a word-spell is given to the person, possibly to be said over the cup while the paper is burning. Sometimes there are restrictions on the spell, requiring that the spell be performed during certain phases of the moon, or that the individual wear a white kerchief on his or her head while performing it, or something similar. These restrictions are given, along with all of the other details of the spell, when the magician who has "fixed" the cup returns it to the one who is to use it.

While this kind of spell is not as elaborate or interesting as the more involved rituals of ceremonial magic, it is often as effective. It is a ritual and ceremonial magic spell however, as it requires the performance of a particular act or ritual, performed in a certain way, and under certain conditions. Once these are fulfilled, it is assumed that the spell will be successful.

I have mentioned that religious ritual eventually degenerates into superstitions of unknown origins. If a superstition is actively believed in by the members of a community, it will hold the same force as a ritual. The superstition will be enforced by the astral power of its believers as strongly as the most formal and solemn ritual of the strongest lodge of ceremonialists on the face of the Earth.

The process of belief in ritual and superstition can best be illustrated by the children's rhyme: "Step on a crack and break your mother's back!" If people subconsciously accept this as a basic belief, violating it with willed and emotional direction will cause as much damage to their mothers as it is possible for their astral force to inflict. This is a simplistic example of the real nature of ritual and ceremonial magic, but it illustrates my point.

Chapter 5

LEARNING RITUAL MAGIC

As with all of the many varieties of occult and spiritual studies, Ritual and Ceremonial Magic is best learned from a teacher who practices it. Until you can locate and be accepted by such a teacher, the following information will assist you in gaining a start on your training. Studying this information, and following it, will be of benefit whether or not you ever find someone to teach you ritual and ceremonial magic. Mastery of these skills will usually make you more acceptable to a teacher should you find one.

The teacher accepts the student, you are not in a position to judge the qualifications of your teacher. There is an old saying about this process: "The wise man can understand the fool because he was once a fool. The fool cannot understand the wise man, since he was never wise." Most of those whom I have met who teach Ritual and Ceremonial Magic teach only their apprentices. Once you master the subject, you may be required to teach two students yourself. As with most of those who teach, you will probably not teach more than two. Tales of large lodges of magicians exist only in fiction.

If you are only seeking an introduction to the subject of Ritual and Ceremonial Magic for intellectual satisfaction there are two books which will give you the knowledge you require, as well as some very practical information. You will be able to practice the art to some extent from these books.

> *Magic: An Occult Primer* by David Conway (New York: E. P. Dutton, 1972) is probably the best introduction to Ritual and Ceremonial Magic in the English language. It is a primer of occult information, with a definite bias toward ritual and ceremonial magic. (The book is now published by Aquarian Press, a division of Harper-Collins in London.)

> *Experimental Magic* by J. H. Brennan (London: Aquarian Press, 1972) is another excellent introduction. Like the former work it was also written by a practicing magician.

As a novice without a teacher you must be particularly cautious about reading any of the popular works of the late Aleister Crowley. These books are not evil, they are just written with tongue in cheek. To an experienced ritual magician some of them, especially Crowley's *Magic*, are quite funny.[1] Crowley intended them to be. The only serious work he wrote was written in his later years in the form of correspondence with a student whom he was seriously trying to teach. This book is *Magic without Tears*.[2] His other works will get a beginner off on the wrong track. His books have ruined more potential magicians than those of any other author.

If you wish to make attainments in the field of Ritual and Ceremonial magic, which you will eventually be able to use to develop yourself spiritually, you need to go about the process with a great deal of caution. Any book you read will place information into your subconscious mind which will have to be unlearned at a later date. The process of unlearning takes much longer and is much more difficult than the process of learning. It's better to develop your mind using the books I mention later in this chapter.

The theory of most so-called "Western Traditional Magic" is based upon the process of releasing the suppressed dynamic power of the subconscious mind by the use of rituals and symbols. The subconscious mind is deliberately trained to relate images to emotions in a

---

[1]Several editions of Crowley's *Magick* have been published. The most recent and complete edition (York Beach, ME: Samuel Weiser, 1994), contains Crowley's own corrections and annotations for a planned second edition never published until now.
[2]The most recent edition of this book was published by New Falcon Publications, Phoenix, AZ, in 1991.

form of auto-hypnosis. This process adds emotional energy to the subconscious mind; it does not remove it. It is very much like the ordinary process of education, where sensory images are connected to images in the subconscious mind through the process of formal education, culture, and childhood experiences. This process is almost the opposite of the spiritually correct procedure of removing emotional blockages from the subconscious mind, and slowly developing a harmony between the conscious and subconscious mind that allows the conscious mind to control, or rather to interrelate with, the dynamic power of the subconscious mind directly.

Serious students must first learn to use their minds. This is accomplished in two steps. First it is necessary to learn how to concentrate the mind so that it may be focused on a subject. Then it is necessary to learn how to meditate. Each step will take at least a year to complete. You will have to go slowly and patiently, day by day, until you have honestly mastered the process. Having done so, you will at least have some potential for attracting a teacher to teach you Ritual and Ceremonial magic. In addition you will find that your approach to life is different, as you have now harnessed your mind to your will, and placed in under your control. This is an achievement which few people ever make. In itself, this is a step in spiritual progress.

The first step in the process of training your mind is to learn to concentrate. Either of the two books below are good guides to concentration. It is important that you do not go on to the next step, meditation, until you have mastered concentration. Real mastery of this art is far more difficult than you may think.

Concentration: An Approach to Meditation, by Ernest Wood (Wheaton, IL: Quest, Theosophical Publishing, 1949).

Concentration: A Guide to Mental Mastery, by Mouni Sadhu (N. Hollywood, CA: Wilshire Book Co., 1959).

Once you have mastered the art of concentrating your mind, you will immediately discover you have a more clear approach to living your life. You will also find that the internal monkey chatter of your mind has stilled, leaving you with more energy to devote to the real process of living.

The second step is learning how to meditate. After mastering the art of concentration, the following book will assist you in learning how to meditate: *Meditation*, by Mouni Sadhu (North Hollywood, CA: Wilshire Book Co., 1978).

These two steps should take you at least two years to complete. Mastery of these two steps will, by themselves, change your life for the better. Your mind will no longer lack direction, and it will be able to work in harmony with the real you. You will be ready for further training at this point. You will also be worth training!

If you can find no training after completing this work, you should continue with your meditation, and also spend about fifteen minutes each day sounding the vowel sounds in your native language in order of their appearance in the alphabet. The voice is one of the magician's most powerful tools, and its training is one of the most important facets of the magician's art. Sounding the vowel sounds is the most frequently given introductory exercise in training ceremonial magicians. Because it seems to have nothing to do with the kind of fantasy that most modern day magicians indulge themselves in, it serves as a screen to dissuade those whose primary interest is self-delusion from those who are actually interested in learning to practice ritual and ceremonial magic.

Assuming you have mastered concentration, spend two years meditating and a year sounding the vowels, you will now have around you sufficient force to draw a teacher to you. If you live in an out of the way place you should make it a point to spend your vacations in large cities, as that is the most likely place for you to meet a teacher. Very few magicians live in small and rural communities in the midwest. A great number live in New York, Chicago, Los Angeles and other major metropolitan centers.

You will probably find your teacher, or at least you will set into motion the chain of events which brings a teacher into your life. In the meantime, you should work on your exercises. The work will pay off in any event.

Chapter 6

DEIFIC
MAGIC

W e now examine practices that believe
that a Deity, a force in the non-physical universe—or a
lesser god—can become interested in intervening in
human affairs. It is called Deific Magic.

Magic may be performed by either a worshiper or a
priest of any religion, although conventional American
Christian religious practice does not expect its
parishioners—or its clergy—to perform magic. In many
cases, the performance of magic is either discouraged or
forbidden by the tenets of the religion. Almost all of the
established religions prefer dealing with the world of
theology and the intellect, and discourage any deviation
from this safe shore to the uncharted wilderness of the
astral and spiritual realms. In these areas, the voice of
the worldly religious hierarchy can exert no control.

There are some religions which demand that priests and clergy be proficient in the practice of magic. The demand for magician-priests is often so strongly made that those priests who cannot successfully perform magic for their parishioners will quickly lose their status as priests, and may even be removed from office. These are the magico-religious practices.

These religions come from ancient times, and emphasize the performance of magic as an integral part of the religious practice. They are religions from what is known as the Sumerian line. They all have roots in, and similarities with, ancient religious practices of Arcadia, Sumeria, Babylonia, and Egypt. These magical religious practices include "deities," creations of the primal creator, usually members of a pantheon, or a group of deities. Like the pantheon of Saints found in the Roman Catholic Church, these deities are appealed to by prayers and offerings, and are asked to assist the worshiper in obtaining worldly desires.

Through the prayers of a worshiper to a deity, saint, or other cult figure, the desires of the member of the religion may often be fulfilled. This is religious magic, or a magico-religious practice. It is a practice of magic very similar to the magico-religious practices of the ancient world, and similar to the religious practices of so-called primitive societies in the world today.

There are many systems of belief in which the actions of deities, beings, or spirits, created by (or emanating from) the Creator God, are viewed as being able to directly influence the incarnate human being. These deities, or emanations, are actually astral forces of the universe which have been anthropomorphized by a particular culture to correspond to the material and emotional requirements of the culture.

The familiar Greek and Roman mythologies are myths of a pantheon of deities that filled a magico-religious need for the living religions of the Greek and Roman societies of ancient times. These Greek and Roman pantheons look a bit pale when compared to the more colorful magico-religious pantheons of some of the African religions, but they are of the same nature.

If we understand deities to be the anthropomorphization of the various forces of the universe, having human attributes in accordance with the needs of the culture in which they serve as deities, they become more comprehensible. The Saints of the Roman Catholic Church are of this nature. In the new world, religious Africans had no difficulty matching their various tribal deities to the Saints of the Roman Catholic Church, and then worshipping them under a new guise.

The parallel between the Catholic saints and the deities of magico-religious pantheons can be carried further. Both saints and deities have rulership over specific areas of human life experience. Both saints and deities are prayed to by their believers for success in the areas of life experience they rule. Believers in both saints and deities have formed cults in honor of these saints and deities. In some cases, there have even evolved formal organizations, with systems of prayers or offerings to both saints and deities. In both cases, some saints or deities are honored more than others. For example, in the Roman Catholic Church there is a St. Jude's league and a number of other prayer organizations, such as the Legion of Mary, the Rosary Society, and so forth. In Santeria there is often a group of devotees of Chango, and other groups honoring other deities. These groups often meet separately to honor their deity, just as the men of St. Jude's league may meet to honor their patron saint separately.

Those who practice deific magic usually believe that every person is born under the rulership of one or two of the deities of their culture's pantheon. This practice may be compared to the Roman Catholic practice of taking the name of a saint when an infant, or when a convert is baptized into the Church. These deities are the spiritual "parents" of the person. It is assumed that they will assist their children in the affairs of their life. Initiation in magico-religious practices usually takes place to the deity who is shown by divination to be the spiritual parent of the initiate.

In Santeria, and in some of the other Afro-Catholic magico-religious practices, the deity closest to the person is referred to as the "owner of the head." The initiation of a person into one of these magico-religious practices is often referred to as the initiate's "giving his or her head" to the deity. In most cases, when the initiation is a valid one, this is just what it is. The initiate has actually had the deity, or at least as much of the deity as he or she can receive, placed into his or her head. From that day forward, the individual's actions, thoughts and beliefs will generally be constrained in accordance with the nature of the deity. Thus an initiate may have a real change of character following initiation. The initiate becomes more uniform in nature, in accordance with the personality of the deity he or she has received.

In addition, the deity of the initiate may choose to use him or her as a trance medium to speak through, or to work through on this Earth. A deity is usually thought to make contact with the people who are "passing them," through the first and second cervical vertebrae, which is located at the back of the neck, just beneath the skull. This point is sometimes referred to as the place where the deity claims ownership of its child.

It is this point, the seat of the deity, that is most strongly affected when the deity "mounts its horse" or takes mediumistic possession (in a trance) of the initiate who is that deity's worshiping child.

There are two magico-religious systems popularly known in the United States. These are the Haitian Voudon or Voodoo practice, originally from the Fon, Rada, and Dahomey peoples of Africa; and the Santeria practice of Cuba, originally from the Yoruba peoples of Nigeria. All of the African magico-religious practices have changed greatly from their African origins in the Americas. These changes have resulted from the exposure of the original African tribal religions to the Western Roman Catholic religion. In addition, the priests of these African religions learned from the various magical and religious practices of Native Americans whom they contacted in the New World, as well as learning from European occultists who came as colonizers.

Native American Shamanism is also a magico-religious system. Indian medicine men, and the spiritual warriors described by Carlos Castanada, are both practitioners of magico-religious systems. They work through, and with, the powerful forces of the universe in the same way that a Santeria Priest or a Voudon Priest does. The paths are similar, although the great differences in culture may make them look very different to the outsider.

Haitian Voudon practices were the basis for most of the many superstitions which permeated Afro-American culture from slave times to the present day. Although they are no longer accepted by the majority of the American black community, these superstitions still influence Afro-American culture to at least some degree. As the practices of Voudon originated in a rural agricultural community in Africa, and as the majority of slave owners in the area of what is now the United States kept the black priesthood in a state of total subjugation, the original religious practices of most African tribal religions were lost in the United States. Only superstition remains in the culture of the American black. An effort is being made by some members of the American African community to revive the religious practices of Africa and apply them to African Americans. We must wait for a few generations to see just how successful this effort actually will be.

In Cuba, the Caribbean, and South America, the Roman Catholic Church enforced a set of Catholic Slave Laws. For all their defects they resulted in a policy toward slaves, both Indian and Black, which was more oriented to maintaining at least a semblance of family life and native culture than was allowed by the less religious slave laws of the colonies which became the United States. Among other things, the Catholic Slave Laws encouraged religious worship among the Blacks. The Catholic Church accepted the Black native priesthood as the spokesman of the slaves, even bringing some of the native African priests into the Roman Catholic Church as deacons, monks, and priests. Unwittingly, the Roman Catholic Church helped keep native African religious practices alive.

In many parts of Spanish-speaking South America there was never any persecution of the black religious, so long as they were able to follow the prescribed Roman Catholic forms of worship to give the appearance of being believing Christians. There are some amazing tales of how the African religious practices were saved for posterity in various countries of South America. Often this was accomplished under the eye of, and even with the unwitting connivance of, the priests of the Roman Catholic Church, itself.

In Haiti, the religious practice of Voudon, which had been the rallying cry assisting the slaves to gain their freedom from the French, developed to a high degree of sophistication despite frequent persecution by both political and religious authority. Voudon is now a fully developed and self-contained magico-religious practice. It has all of the attributes of any other religion, complete with at least parts of a graded ecclesiastical authority.

Santeria in Cuba has achieved the same place, as have the allied Macumba and Candomble religious practices of Brazil and Central America. Since the Cuban Revolution of Castro, the focus of the Santeria religion has shifted from Cuba to Miami and New York. Santeria and its sister form, Lucumi, are thriving in these new sites. There are now large groups of both worshipers and initiates who have neither a Spanish nor an African background.

As the United States is a melting pot nation, we might expect to find a variety of other magico-religious systems here which represent cultures other than African. In fact, we do. The Pennsylvania Dutch Hex practice, centered in Lancaster County, Pennsylvania, is probably the best-known example. This Christian magical practice takes its origin from Franconian Switzerland, located about 240 miles southwest of Berlin. The first Pennsylvania Dutch Hex service in America was held about sunset on December 24, 1694, on the bank of the Delaware River in Philadelphia. In a few of the old line rural Dutch or German communities, these hex services, which mark the solstices with a bonfire festival, are held to this day.

Other magico-religious practices found in the United States include the Italian Strega practice and the Scandinavian Odinist practices. The Italian Strega practice comes from Italy and Sicily, while the Odinist practice is better known in Iceland than in most of Scandinavia at the present time. All of these practices have a great deal in common with each other, and all have been greatly distorted because of their contact with more conventional American religions.

The Christian Satanic practice, although it is not really as widespread as popular literature would have you think, is another practice of deific magic. Most Christians look for salvation in the world to come, a world or heaven opened to them because of Christ's sacrifice. The Christian Satanic believer exchanges the world to come for the hope of material power on Earth. They do this by formally or ritually surrendering their Christian salvation to Satan, promising to serve the will of Satan instead of following Christ. In their worship services, Satanists practice rites that are opposed to Christian theological concepts. They do this to demonstrate their dedication to Satan, and their turning from the salvation promised by Christ. Using a nude woman as the altar for their worship, and practicing orgiastic promiscuous copulation with other members of their group are the kind of anti-Christian ritual actions that Satanists practice. As animal sacrifice is not a part of Christianity, a true Satanist would be indifferent to it.

When people are native to a magico-religious system they literally learn the religion with their mother's milk. There are no subsequent inhibitions or blockages within that make it difficult for their astral natures to fulfill the goals which they pray for. There is no hesitation within them when making a request of a deity, or in expecting the fulfillment of the request. They learn the nature of the pantheon and of the various deities in earliest childhood, accepting the dogmas of the religion with the unquestioning acceptance of a child. Their conscious and subconscious minds are in agreement in all things connected with the practice of the religion.

As these individuals grow to adulthood, they will have many examples of the efficacy of the religious practice presented to them. They will learn with sure and certain knowledge, as an example, that if they place five red flowers before a statue of the deity who rules headaches, their headache will be cured. They will become familiar with the rituals and practices of the religion, and they will accept the process of magic as a part of their religion.

These people will also learn that not all of the processes of deific magic are simple. They will understand that more complex requests require more complex offerings. In some cases these offerings must be made by priests of the deity to whom the request is made. They understand that some offerings are not acceptable when made by an ordinary worshiper.

In some cases, people who desire to make an offering may not be certain that the deity will look with favor on their requests. They know that sometimes the deity responds favorably to requests from worshipers, while at other times the request is not fulfilled. There is a danger of uncertainty present, depending upon the request being made. In no society, and in no culture is all magical procedure foolproof.

Because an element of chance exists when making a major request of a deity, there must be a way of determining whether a particular deity will grant the believer's request. The way the desires of any deity are revealed is through the process of divination. Through divination, made by either a diviner or a priest, the will of the deity is known before the request is made. Generally, the priest will make the divination for more general requests, while in the case of initiations, and in the case of major specific requests, the professional diviner is consulted.

In some divinations, the offerings required by the deity are revealed as a result of the divination. Some magico-religious practices have an agreed upon system of offerings and divinations which is so regularized that some of them have even been published. In other systems, the diviner has to be an initiated priest of the deity of the "oracle" or the deity of "fate." The diviner usually has great influence over the body of the priesthood in the religion. The office of diviner-priest usually requires that the diviner memorize a huge body of divinations, each of which apply to specific cases, and each of which relate to specific offerings for the various deities.

The offering to be given to the deity may be regarded as payment to the deity for the work which is to be performed by the deity. In most systems of magico-religious practice, an offering is required for every request made of a deity. The five red flowers in the example mentioned earlier were assumed to be the standard offering to alleviate a petitioner's headache.

In the eyes of the worshiper, the process of divination for diagnosis, and propitiation through offerings and prayer, set up an almost foolproof system for controlling the variables of life. When this procedure is followed by a sincerely believing worshiper who is native to the culture, it allows the full astral force of the worshiper to act favorably on any request he or she happens to make.

In many of the African magico-religious practices, the office of priest and diviner are separated; the diviner is consulted only about more important questions in the life of the worshiper. Consultations with the diviner may or may not result in offerings being given to a deity. In some cases, consultation with a diviner has no other purpose than obtaining general guidance.

Systems such as this, typical of most magico-religious practices, have an element of guarantee present. There is no reason for the petitioner to feel that his or her request will not be well received. Any mental inhibitions against the application of the full astral force of the individual is eliminated through the process of divination and offering.

These magico-religious systems work well for their worshipers. Their effectiveness in giving their believers what they want, in terms of healing the body and guiding the life, is why they are so attractive to those who have not been born into them. More conventional religions condemn these magico-religious practices because of their successes, not because they do not serve their worshipers. The fact that the practice is successful is what makes the magico-religious practice threatening to the more conventional religions.

Magico-religious practices promise other things that more conventional religions do not offer their worshipers. First, in most of the more widely known of the practices, any worshiper can become a priest or priestess without the necessity of going through a time-consuming formal process of intellectual education. In most practices, all that is required is a basic initial training and an initiation. While the initiation is expensive, it is not unreasonably so. Once a person becomes a priest of the religion he or she has a status in the community which is difficult to match otherwise. In addition, there is usually the possibility of earning at least a small income from being a priest.

Second, a member of the religion, and more especially a priest, has the feeling of being the possessor of occult powers, secrets, and truths not available to the common people. The festivals of the religion bring the worshiper in touch with another world very graphically. Being addressed by a medium possessed of a deity is an experience which even the most hardened rationalist is not likely to forget. Being possessed by either a spirit or a deity is also an experience which one is not likely to forget. The attendance at a magico-religious festival, even for a person who is not a member of the religion, is often a life-changing event.

It is difficult for those in the community not to regard those who are the priests of a deity as being people set apart from the common herd. These priests often give the ordinary worshiper tasks to do to solve life problems which make the worshiper feel that he or she is at least participating in a magical act, if not developing the ability to perform magic. In some cases this is true, and in some cases it is not, but the worshiper gains status from the action none the less.

The participatory nature of the magico-religious practices also has a great attraction for the worshiper. In almost all of these practices the festivals of religious worship are much more like parties than solemn religious ceremonies. They are really enjoyable social occasions, and all who attend participate. Festivals are never solemn or formal services, and they are never limited to preaching. In communities where these religious practices are in the majority the last festival is talked of for months afterward. The coming festival is always anticipated eagerly.

Deific magic practices in the "Spanish Harlems" of our larger cities and in the rural areas of Puerto Rico and Haiti become more comprehensible when they are understood this way. Aside from being a magico-religious practice, these religions fill all of the areas in the life of the people which could be filled by any other religious practice. In addition, the priest provides counsel and solutions to the problems of everyday life, serving the role of both physician and psychiatrist in the community.

In the more formal and community based magico-religious practices, deific magic is usually taught to potential priests on a one-to-one basis. Teacher and students engage in a close personal relationship over a long period of time. This type of relationship is similar to the one written about by Carlos Castanada in his books about *Don Juan*, and in the book *Medicine Woman* and others by Lynn V. Andrews. The relationship culminates in the teacher initiating the students. In the actual initiation, the teacher essentially gives students the use of the astral force which the students have – through the guidance of the teacher – developed within themselves.

Most of the teaching of the intricacies of the practice is based upon the belief system of the magico-religious practice. The technology of the magical practice itself is also taught, something which often takes very little time. For people born into the culture, in most practices the training rarely takes less than two years. In other practices however, the training can be for as long as twenty years.

Training is more direct among those who have the belief system of the deific magico-religious practice as a part of their environment. Their natural belief system is only reinforced by the detailed training students receive from the priest who is their teacher. In this, the process of training is much the same as the process of religious training.

Even though conversions are frequently made, there is little chance of truly successful conversions from any of the more conventional American religious belief systems to any of the Afro-Catholic magico-religious practices. Such conversions usually produce subconscious mental turmoil in the converts, originating in the disparity of the belief systems. Valid conversions are only possible when there is a strong similarity between the fundamental beliefs.

A Spanish-speaking American of Spanish descent who was a Roman Catholic by birth and education would have little difficulty converting to an African based magico-religious system having a strong Spanish Roman Catholic base, such as the Santeria or Lecumi religions of the Caribbean and the Condemble or Macumba religious practices of Central and South America. An American Protestant Baptist traveling to Africa to obtain initiation into an African tribal religion is unlikely to ever be able to reconcile the beliefs of childhood with what will be learned in the conversion process. It is unlikely that the conversion would ultimately be really effective. In this case there are simply too many discrepancies between childhood religious practice and the newly learned magico-religious practice. These discrepancies form a block of inhibitions against converts using their astral force successfully in performing the rituals of the new practice. This means that converts may have difficulty developing the ability to perform magic.

To make effective conversions from one religion to another, the mind of the converts must be rid of all apparent and real impediments to the belief structure of the religion to which they are converting. This must be done before the actual process of conversion occurs. The practice of the new religion must be learned in the same way that a ceremonial magician would learn the practice. Mental exercises freeing the mind from inhibitions, guilts, and fears of all kinds must prepare students for the imposition of a new belief structure.

Ideally, the new belief structure, along with the intricacies and technicalities of the new religion, should be learned as a tool. In this way it becomes one of many means of approaching reality, rather than the only way of approaching it. This is not ever an easy task for converts, as it is quite difficult to unlearn the childhood religion and replace it with a new one. It is always more difficult to learn a new religious belief for it involves the interaction of both the conscious and subconscious minds. When people learn a new metaphysical system, the learning process usually involves only the conscious mind.

In almost all religions, God and the deities (if any) are viewed as having the power to reward and punish mankind. Changes of religious practice to a practice forbidden by the childhood religion will usually call forth the punishment of "God," through the agency of the person's own subconscious mind. This punishment actually voids the conversion process.

Many magico-religious systems promise power to those who are initiated. Whether or not this gain of power actually occurs is another question. Whatever power may be achieved is always power native to the individual. Initiation usually results in a focusing of the individual's astral power. The ability to focus is a result of the initiation. It is not really a gain of astral power. For a convert, the power is lessened by the convert's inability to completely accept the new religious practice because of social and cultural divergences from previous belief patterns. This difficulty is particularly important when there is a great conflict between the original beliefs and the beliefs of the new religious practice, for example the conversion from conservative Protestant fundamentalism to an Afro-Catholic magico-religious practice.

It requires a great deal of mental training to make a successful conversion to any magico-religious practice. Unfortunately, most practitioners of the better known magico-religious practices are not really able to guide a student through such training because the practitioners who do the most initiating are usually native to the system, and in their native culture such extensive mental training is not required.

Before you decide that a quick conversion to a magico-religious practice will give you all of the power you could ever want, you should bear these facts in mind. Before considering such a conversion you should take time to examine yourself and investigate your motives. When you are sure that you want to make the conversion, you must look hard enough to find a group actively practicing in a way which will fit in with your idea of what such groups should be. No matter what you may have heard, every "family" of a magico-religious group is different, and actual practices are as different as families are.

A magico-religious practice of a more familiar sort is found in the Roman Catholic practice of praying to the saints. If you are a Roman Catholic, you already have a magico-religious practice which you may put to good use whenever you wish. You can obtain books of attributions of the saints, and get a list of their feast days. Then all you have to do is pick out the saints you decide you want to work with, based upon their attributions, or rulerships. Saints' names in your given name, or any particular saint you feel close to, are good places to start.

I knew a young man whose first names were Michael Christopher. He was raised Catholic, but fell away from the church because he did not feel that there was any power in the mass anymore. After sixteen years of Roman Catholic education, he subconsciously was firmly convinced of the value of the religion in his life, but consciously he wanted to develop himself by becoming a magician. He was interested in Santeria, and he had a reading by a Santero, who told him that they would welcome him to join the religion as an initiate.

However, he really was a Roman Catholic, and he eventually started doing daily devotions to his name saints, Saint Michael and Saint Christopher, instead. Over the last few years he has been able to accomplish several good things through working with these saints. As one example, after getting laid off from his job in a corporate downsizing, he was offered a better job in what he thought was his last elevator ride from the job he was leaving. He had prayed that if he was hit by the downsizing, he would be able to obtain employment immediately. St. Christopher made certain that he obtained even better employment than he previously had.

On the other hand, I know a man with a nominally Jewish background who heads a Santeria family. His conversion worked, and was effective, and he is considered to be one of the leading Santero Priests in his area. Most of the initiated members of his family are from only nominally religious backgrounds, and they are all quite successful in their practice of the Santeria religion.

Chapter 7

COMMUNING WITH THE SPIRITS

When King Saul consulted the woman of Endor (I Samuel 28:7-25), he was consulting a woman who worked with the spirits of the dead. Technically, she was a necromancer, as that is what a person who works with the spirits of dead people is called.

7—Then said Saul unto his servants, Seek me a woman that hath a familiar spirit, that I may go to her, and enquire of her. And his servants said to him, Behold, there is a woman that hath a familiar spirit at Endor.

8—And Saul disguised himself, and put on other raiment, and he went, and two men with him, and they came to the woman by night: and

> he said, I pray thee, divine unto me by the
> familiar spirit, and bring me him up, whom I
> shall name unto thee.
>
> 9 – And the woman said unto him, Behold, thou
> knowest what Saul hath done, how he hath cut
> off those that have familiar spirits, and the wiz-
> ards, out of the land: wherefore then layest
> thou a snare for my life, to cause me to die? (1
> Samuel 28: 7–9).

The purpose of Saul's consultation was to gain information, not for the performance of magic. Obtaining information from the spirits of the dead, and using spirits to
perform magic, both fall under the general heading of
working with spirits of the dead, or necromancy. It is an
entirely different form of magical practice than any
which we have considered previously.

Working with spirits presupposes that they are
accessible, in some way, to the living. It also presupposes that spirits have sufficient interest in those who
are still living to be willing to assist them in their daily
life. The belief that these spirits are accessible to the
living, and that they are interested in the living, is
accepted to this day by many so-called primitive cultures. For example, the ancient Celtic peoples treated
the spirits of their dead in this way. The Celts invited
their dead relatives to actively participate in the daily
life of the living family. The practice of revering ancestors, which has been carried on by pre-revolutionary
Chinese for many centuries, is also well known.

In the earliest years of Christianity, the deceased
members of the family, and deceased friends, were
called on to pray for the living, just as the living prayed

for the dead. This was especially true in the case of close relatives, who were asked to pray for the success as well as for the salvation of those who were still living. The dearly departed were even asked to pray for the living on their memorials and the legend appearing on many older tombstones carries this request. It was only natural that the dearly departed should be looked to for guidance by those who were still living.

Prayers to the spirits are no more unusual than prayers of veneration, or the requests for help and guidance that are offered to saints and martyrs of the Christian church. In the case of immediate ancestors, it is likely that they will maintain an interest in the lives of those whom they knew when they were alive. The implied interest of the spirits in the affairs of the living is one of the reasons why prayers and offerings are made to ancestors. This practice is found in many societies throughout the world. In more remote areas, and among more so-called primitive societies, prayers to the ancestors, and even occasional ancestor worship, is common.

Making prayers to ancestors has similarities with more formal magical practices. Ancestors are frequently treated in the same way as are living members of the family. In some cultures and in some societies, this is more noticeable than in others. In some, offerings are made to ancestors every day at an ancestral shrine located in the home. Ancestors are often included in discussions of family affairs, much as are the living members of the family. Through this directed interest of the living in the dead, the ancestors are asked to assist living members of the family in making progress in their lives. Often specific questions are asked the dead, and in some cultures it is believed that the departed ancestors reply to these questions through dreams.

Those who work with the spirits of the dead usually find that it is easier to work with the spirits of those who had an interest in them while they were alive. It is necessary to maintain the friendly relationship between the living person and the deceased. This is probably why ancestor worship, or more accurately, ancestor remembrance, is so widespread. It seems to have beneficial effects on those families who practice it.

The woman of Endor was not a special case, for many people work with spirits to obtain information from them. In our society many people use Ouija boards, or we find trance mediums in Spiritualist Churches, and many so-called "new age" mediums seem to produce limitless amounts of "channeled" information. Working with spirits, along these lines anyway, is almost a respectable form of occult practice in the United States.

The woman of Endor used a somewhat more sophisticated device than either a spiritualistic trance or a Ouija board. Hers was a device which had been in use for thousands of years before King Saul made his fateful decision to consult a woman with a familiar spirit. According to the Hebrew text, Saul instructed his servants to find a woman who possessed an Oboth. The Oboth or Ob, is a oracular head. At one time, many years before King Saul was born, the oracular head was especially made from the physical head taken from the body of the ritually sacrificed "sacred" King.

Oracular heads are still made in various parts of the world, in accordance with the requirements of the practices that still use them. The heads are usually replaced with other, similar, instruments in the more modern magical practices that involve working with spirits. The Govi used to keep a departed spirit on an altar in the

Voudon practice, and the iron cauldron used in the Palo practice associated with Santeria are similar devices. In our society it would be difficult to have a talking head sitting around the house. A covered pot or a jar causes casual visitors little concern.

Oracular heads, and their modern equivalents, are made according to strict but secret rules. That there is no real reason for this secrecy can be demonstrated once it is realized that the specific rules vary widely among different practices. The heads are almost always formed on the cleaned skull and first two vertebra (atlas and axis) of the deceased person. The interior of the skull is filled with a variety of things, usually herbs and other ingredients, while the outside of the skull is molded with clay to resemble the living person from whom it was taken. At a minimum the skull is covered with clay and made to resemble a living person. The physical construction of the oracular head is similar in all of the practices with which I am familiar. Unless the head is made by someone who has both artistic and magical talent, it is usually a bit macabre.

Oracular heads, like the pot of the Palaro, are used primarily for communication with the spirits of the dead. Their purpose is always communication rather than the performance of magic. The Govi of the Voudon practice is quite similar, in that it is used to communicate with the ancestor who is said to "live" in it. These instruments are not primarily used for the performance of magic; for magical work another device is required.

In 1 Samuel 28:9, the original Hebrew text quotes the woman of Endor replying to Saul, "Behold, you know what Saul has done, he has cast off those who have the Oboth and the Yiddeonim from the land." The Oboth is the instrument used for divination, and the

Yiddeonim is the device used for gaining the magical remedy desired through the work of the spirits. This follows the usual magical formula of diagnosis through divination and remedy through magic which we have seen operate in various magico-religious practices. It is Yiddeonim which is translated as "wizards" in the King James version of the Bible. As both these instruments had fallen into disuse in official Judaism, and were never a part of Christianity, the translators who translated the Old Testament from Hebrew into Greek about 100 B.C. did not know what these two words meant. As in many other places in the Bible, they translated them as well as they could. Like the Oboth, the Yiddeonim is a manufactured or fabricated device particular to the culture and the magical tradition of the person making it.

In modern times the Yiddeonim is often an iron pot, or even a large cauldron, which contains an assortment of materials. It can also be a wooden box, like an old cigar box, which contains an assortment of things. The form it takes depends entirely on the practice of the person using it. In most European practices, it is a very ordinary assortment of things in a wooden box. It may contain a photograph of the spirit when alive and an announcement of his or her death. It may contain mass cards for masses said for the repose of the soul. It may contain other mementos of the person—wedding rings, a rosary or something similar.

Whatever physical form these psychic instruments take, they serve a purpose in the realm of the spirit as well as in the physical realms. The head serves as an earthly residence for the spirit of the oracle, while the box, pot, or jar containing the materials associated with the "working" spirit serves as a homing device for it. We might even say that it is a beacon light for both the magician and the spirit which the magician uses in his or her work. It can be seen in both the physical and astral worlds, giving the spirit a place to receive instruction from the magician, and claim the reward when the work is completed.

In the Palo and Muyombrero practices associated with the Santeria magico-religious practice, these instruments are usually iron cauldrons containing an assortment of materials. Offerings to the spirits for the successful completion of their work are placed in the cauldron. Within a few months or so of beginning to work with the dead, the cauldron can become a bit "ripe" from decaying food offerings, sacrifices, and other assorted things added to it.

If the magician is working with only one spirit, the focus may be a symbol of the spirit being worked with. For example, a doll or a statue may be used for this purpose. In Egypt, statues had small holes in them, so they could hold secret magical ingredients. A magician working with a number of spirits might use a number of dolls, each of them a focus for one spirit.

This use of specially prepared dolls is found in Africa today, as well as in Jamaica and Brazil. The exact composition of the focus, the Yiddeonim, like the exact composition of the Oboth, is the secret of the practice in which the magician works. In some cases the secret of their manufacture is so well kept that only certain leaders of the practice are allowed to make items that will be used by ordinary practitioners.

If we compare the practice of working with spirits to the more familiar practice of mediumship, as it is found in our modern society, we could compare the Oboth or Oracular head and the Ouija board. Both are devices used to gain information from the dead. If the people using the Ouija board have a good spirit working with them, they can obtain quite accurate information. The same is true of people using an oracular head, or other focus for an information-gathering spirit.

The practice of mediumship, when an individual is possessed by spirits or deities, is actually a bit different. In the case of the Spiritist movement in South America, mediums have performed healings while in a spiritualistic trance. In the case of Spiritist mediums, both the information and the magic come from the same source. The magic performed in spiritist assemblies, however, is almost always limited to curing physical conditions of the people being treated.

The spiritist movement is a magico-religious practice to at least this extent, although I have never been able to identify a deity pantheon in the practice. While there are some spirits which seem to appear at a number of the many spiritist groups, there are also unique spirits in each of the groups. The mediums in spiritist groups are almost always dedicated and sincere people. They are a good cut or two above the type of medium that you would meet in spiritualist churches and their summer camps.

The shamanistic tradition of mediums passing spirits and deities is found in many magico-religious practices. This is one of the more popularly recognized features of both the Voudon practice and Santeria. When in possession by a deity, a medium can perform feats which not only amaze and mystify onlookers but which would qualify as miracles in every sense of the word.

Again, this work may be considered working with spirits of the dead, but it is actually a part of the belief of the magico-religious practice involved. It is considered to be working with spirits only because the magico-religious practices usually believe that the power of their deities comes from the spirits of those who were the priests and priestesses of the deity while they were alive. In some magico-religious practices, initiation is referred to as "giving one's head" to the deity to which the person is initiated. In fact, in a valid initiation in these practices, it is just that; the person actually gives himself or herself to the deity.

In the realm of mediumship it must be noted that there are many degrees and stages of mediumship. Some mediums do a considerably better job of "passing their spirit" than others. There are also various types of mediumship. Some mediums are instruments for pro-ducing physical effects. Other mediums only dance while they are in the mediumistic trance. Still other mediums allow the deity to communicate directly with people, who consult them with questions and listen to their advice, while the medium is in trance.

There are a large number of fraudulent mediums who have learned to successfully fake a trance. They seem to be passing through messages from the dear departed to their credulous audience. Playing on the sympathy of those upon whom they prey, these so-called mediums have brought the whole business of spiritism and mediumship into a bad light. There are "Psychical Research Societies" both in England and the United States that specialize in investigating and exposing fraudulent mediums of this type.

Spirits of the dead are no more wise when they are dead than they were when they were alive! We do not gain great knowledge simply through the process of dying. The dead have the same beliefs and prejudices they held when they were alive. Death does not change spirits except for bringing a slight change in perspective. Even the most skeptical dead will believe in an existence after death.

Spirits can travel around their city or rural neighborhood without being seen by most people. Most spirits have some ability to see into the future, but usually only along the line of probability. How far spirits can see, and how clearly they can see, is a matter for individual spirits. Most spirits are not good at either seeing very far, or seeing very clearly. Many spirits are great braggarts, and will play vicious tricks on people who can communicate with them but who are credulous. Many of these seriously deluded people ascribe great powers to the trickster spirits who prey on them.

It is not enough to just contact spirits, it takes a great deal of time to find out if they can provide you with any useful information. Most spirits just cannot do so. It is beyond their ability. Most spirits cannot perform magic either, much less do all of the wonderful things that many of them will tell you they can do when you contact them. Working with the dead, like all other modes of magic, can be a rather tricky business. Magic always requires a great deal of discrimination, separating "what is" from what you "desire to be." There is not any easy way to work magic.

The ability to speak with the dead must first be developed before you can work with them successfully. If you do not have this ability, you will make no progress with this form of magic. As with any other serious occult study, the study of necromancy requires that you work and study with a teacher who actually works with the dead. Magic worked with spirits (necromancy) is a very powerful and worthwhile form of magical practice if you have the ability. If your tendencies, thoughts, and feelings seem a bit morbid to most people, you may have a natural bent for this form of magical practice. If this is the case, you will probably find that it will be a great deal easier to practice than ceremonial magic. You will also find that necromancy is a good deal more powerful for most practical work.

People who would like to begin to work favorably with their ancestors can follow the following program. You may find that you will have some response from them, but you may also find that you do not receive any response. You should not seek a verbal response, as you may have a response only as a favorable change in your life. It is also quite possible that you will have no response at all.

If you stick to the program given below you will find that it will probably be beneficial for you in your life in any event. Being kind to your ancestral spirits usually is a worthwhile thing to do. This is why so many cultures follow a similar practice.

First: Obtain as detailed a list as possible of your ancestors. You should attempt to learn as much as you can about them, and find out how they were connected by ties of friendship and common interests. Pick two or three ancestors who you either have pictures of, or can obtain pictures of. These should be ancestors from this list. These are the ancestors with whom you will work.

Second: At least every week you should light a candle to each of them, a small birthday candle will do, and ask them for help and guidance in your life. After you do this you should place a glass of cold water in front of each of the pictures, one glass for each picture, and thank them for their assistance in your life.

Third: Keep doing this each week for at least six months; it usually takes that long to begin to make any kind of real contact. In the meantime, if you think you hear your ancestors speaking to you, avoid talking to them. Just keep making the offerings and asking for help and guidance in your life and thanking them for the help and guidance they are giving you.

The reason you are avoiding speaking to them is that the voices you may hear are probably trickster spirits, and not your ancestors at all. Despite any belief you may have that you can tell the difference, you will not be able to do so. So just ignore the voices and keep making the offerings.

After a year or so you will probably find that you are beginning to get good inspirations from these spirits. The proof of this is that your life is now running in a more smooth manner, with less trauma. If this is the case keep up the weekly offerings. If it is not, you may make the offerings less frequently, or even discontinue them.

Chapter 8

LEARNING ASTRAL PROJECTION

Astral projection is a technique which may be used by magicians working in any magical practice but astral projection is not a magical practice in itself. It is certainly one of the most useful techniques available to magicians. Once magicians master true astral projection, there is no barrier of space which can prevent them from learning whatever they desire to know. Astral projection is not a means of divination; it does not describe the future. It is a technique that allows those who practice it to learn about the present.

Astral projection, called by some authors etheric projection, is a technique for using the astral form (or astral body) to explore both the astral and physical worlds. Magicians who are able to develop their talent to the highest degree can use astral projection to make changes in the physical world.

Astral projection usually occurs on a spontaneous basis in those who are passing through adolescence. The experience is usually so frightening to young people that the emotion of fear, which it manifests within them, is sufficient to close down the faculty indefinitely. However, if the first spontaneous experience of astral projection is successful and is encouraged, the ability may be developed and used later.

Astral projection is based upon the concept that human beings have a number of nonphysical bodies. The physical body, in this view, is understood to be the most dense and least subtle of the bodies. The astral body is the next body above the physical body. It is thought to be less dense and more subtle than the physical body. The mental body is more subtle than the astral body, while the spiritual body is the least dense and the most subtle of all of the bodies. The theory of astral projection is that people may separate the astral body and part of the mental consciousness from the gross physical body. It is believed that when this occurs people are still connected to their physical bodies, as only a part of the astral body separates from the physical body. Different schools have different details in their explanations of the many questions and details which surround this nonphysical process.

There are several organizations that attempt to teach astral projection to their students. These groups have a varying degree of success. Eckankar, one of these organizations, claims to be a spiritual group of great antiquity. They occasionally have success in developing the basic ability to project astrally in a few of their students. They have a great deal of written material available to members of their organization.

Like any other arcane art, astral projection is best taught on a one-to-one basis by a teacher who is proficient at the art. I mentioned earlier that not every person can learn to project the astral body. In most cases the art can be taught only on a very limited basis; for example, students may learn to project their astral bodies only in the space of their bedrooms.

Because of the obvious value of astral projection in exploring the nonphysical realms of being, it has been adopted as a technique by some people are not really proficient at projection. Those who "explore the astral" but who cannot explore the earthly realms are indulging in self-delusion and fantasy. It is quite possible to project a fantasy of their "astral experiences" and even involve a number of others in it. The difference between astral projection and fantasy is that, as with other forms of magic, concrete results may be obtained with true astral projection. These materially manifested results are insisted on by those who actually teach the art, before students are allowed to enter into any of the "astral" realms. Only after students have demonstrated that they are ready is astral exploration encouraged.

Once students are able to leave their physical bodies and navigate successfully with the astral body in the immediate environment, they are instructed in methods of traveling increasing distances on Earth. They must also master the process of successfully returning to the physical body on command. Once these basic steps are mastered, students begin practicing the control of physical objects with their astral form. The first exercise is usually something relatively simple, like knocking a balanced playing card to the floor from the edge of a table. Once this simple exercise is perfected, the complexity of the exercises is gradually increased, with the student being required to master each exercise before another is assigned.

Eventually, the best students will be able to move a weight of about fifty pounds, or up to about a third of their body weight, using their astral forms. When students are consistently able to accomplish this, they are ready to begin the process of learning how to perform magic with the astral body.

When young people project spontaneously at puberty they are usually interested in either having sex, or watching sex, while the projector is traveling in the physical realm. This is a negative practice in that it is a waste of energy. It can also lead directly to using the faculty of astral projection for fantasy and self-delusion. Astral sex should be avoided for reasons of emotional stability, if not for reasons of common morality.

When people indulge in astral sex, they often believe that those who have been their astral sex partners are consciously aware of the astral encounter. This is not only not true, but the astral encounter can actually be rather frightening to the supposed partner. In some cases the partner may have been aware of the astral sexual encounter on the level of the deep subconscious. His or her awareness of this encounter, which has not entered the conscious mind, may cause the individual to react negatively to the person who holds the conscious memory of the astral event.

Once students have mastered the ability of moving fairly large weights with the astral body, they can be assured that they can accomplish things in the astral realms which will have a real physical result. This is demonstrated by deliberately manipulating forms in a closed and locked room at a distance from the projecting students. Next students begin leaving written messages for their teachers. The message is left in a physically closed and locked room. Other similar, and increasingly complex, tasks are assigned by the teacher as students grow more proficient at these simple tasks.

With the correctly developed ability to project astrally, individuals can accomplish anything which they could do if they were physically present in the room where the task is to be accomplished. The primary advantage of astral projection is the apparent invisibility of the person who is performing the tasks.

Once the earthly realms have been adequately explored, students can then gradually proceed to the exploration of the astral realms. By having devoted so much time to the exploration of the earthly world they have learned to project a great deal of the "self" with them into the astral body. In addition, they are quite confident of their ability to interact with whatever they may encounter.

A great deal of trash has been written about exploring the astral realms. I do not intend to add to it. The astral realms are very different from the realm of Earth, and one has to learn a new set of rules and references to get along in them. Having the ability to project on Earth will teach students most of these rules in a relatively painless manner. The astral realms are neither as wonderful or as horrible as they have been described in literature.

The projection of human consciousness is a good part of the projection of the astral body. Unless more is projected than the consciousness, little may be accomplished by projection. It is much simpler to develop your abilities of fantasy and self-deception than it is to develop the ability to project consciousness. In the realms of fantasy and self-deception you can see what you wish to see, whether the desire to see originates from either your conscious or subconscious mind.

When people project the astral body consciously into the astral realms, they learn that things do not always work out according to their desires. Further, they usually see things that they truly do not wish to see. In many cases, this astral projection may destroy some fondly held beliefs and opinions. It requires a certain state of being, both mental and emotional, to attain the goal of entering successfully the astral realms, much less working there.

Entering the physical realm astrally also brings a different view of the world. When entering the astral realms, preconceptions, beliefs, and assumptions act as effective barriers to prevent people from learning anything that they are not ready to learn. In the astral body, it is difficult to indulge in fantasy and self-delusion about the physical world. No such barrier exists in the astral realms, where thoughts create reality, based upon both conscious and subconscious desires.

The trap of entering unprepared into the astral realms is similar to the drug-induced experiences reported in psychological journals and the popular press. The difference between the "good trips" and the "bad trips" are the differences between the individual's astral reality at the time of the drug experience. In magical training there is no use for the drug-induced astral experience, except to point out the similarity of dangers to the unprepared in projection to the astral realms.

Before students enter the astral realms, they must be able to project a great deal of their astral force under their conscious control. This always requires a clear, focused and concentrated mind. The projecting people must also be able to use their sensory organs at the astral level. Just as children do not automatically understand how to use sensory organs at birth, students must learn to operate in this new non-physical environment. The easiest way to do so is through learning to operate in the astral form in the familiar environment of Earth.

Students must be able to project a great deal of "themselves" with them when they leave the familiar sphere of Earth to visit the astral. If they project only their minds they will not be able to accomplish anything in the astral realms except engage in fantasy. Self-delusion is the constant companion of those who desire to work in the astral spheres. It is always necessary to take these exercises one step at a time, with a teacher who can correctly guide students.

Being able to project astrally does not open up a vast field of splendors. It simply makes it possible to learn more about forces that influence the Earth sphere. It will take a great deal of experience in projecting to the astral realms before you are able to begin to influence or control these powerful forces. Like anything else, mastering astral projection, whether on Earth or in the astral realms, is more perspiration than inspiration. While astral projection is a very useful technique, in reality it is not achieved by many people and it is not achieved easily.

Learning to Project Your Astral Body

Once you are able to totally relax your physical body, and have mastered the other exercises given in the chapter "Preparing Yourself to Practice Magic," you can attempt to project your astral body. It is most important that you do not become disappointed if you are not immediately successful at projecting. Most people are not successful at the first conscious attempt at projecting. If you are not immediately successful, you should just keep on trying.

If you want to project astrally, you must begin by totally relaxing your physical body. The best place for your first attempt at projection of your astral body is in your bedroom. Lock the door. You should always relax yourself for astral projection in a place where you will not be disturbed. Once your body is completely relaxed, you should focus your mind on sitting up in your bed. Feel yourself sit up, just as you would if you were sitting up in your physical body, but do not let your physical body move.

Once you feel that you are sitting up, open your eyes without moving your physical eyes. Just make the same effort in a non-physical manner. Either you will be able to see your feet, the feet of your physical body, or you will not. If you can see the feet of your physical body, you have successfully projected at least partly out of your body astrally. If you do not project, relax yourself even deeper and attempt to project again. Don't give up; some people try many times before they succeed.

Now comes the hard part. You must now lie back down in your physical body and relax your body even deeper, and then you must project into a sitting up position again. You should do this several times. You may keep your astral eyes open when you do this, but you should keep your physical eyes closed. You are attempting to master projecting into a sitting position, nothing more. Once you have been successful in several attempts, you should quit for the day.

The following day you should repeat the above exercise several more times. You can add to this sitting projection. You can look at your hands and arms, as they are projected from your body with your trunk, and you can flex the fingers of the astral body. Each time you sit up astrally, you are working toward mastering the art of astral projection. Just as an infant does not immediately start walking without difficulty, you should not expect immediate success in your projection. You will have at least as many failures as successes at first, but you must persist to overcome the failures with constant success. Only when you are consistently able to sit up in your astral body will you be able to master the art of projection in the physical plane.

Once you have mastered sitting up, looking at your hands and arms, and flexing your fingers, you are ready to get completely out of your body. To do this, just swing your astral body to the side of the bed, as you would if you were getting out of bed physically. Place your feet firmly on the floor, and remember that the floor is not solid to you now. Stand up and walk around your bedroom, then get back into your body and perform this simple action again. You must perfect your ability at getting in and out of your physical body before you go any further.

Once you have mastered the art of getting in and out of your body, you should master walking around your bedroom, peering into closets and so forth in your astral body before you attempt to leave the safety of your bedroom. You must master these things, because they all require concentration and a clear mind. It is far better that you do this in your bedroom, alone, than to be distracted by the sights and sounds of others while you are learning to handle your astral body.

Earlier I used the example of an infant learning to walk. This is a good example, as you are in the same position that an infant is in when it is learning to walk. Your supposedly familiar environment is now foreign and strange, as you are not in the familiar physical body which you have learned to use so well. You are in your astral body, which has different characteristics and a different requirement for motion and control. It will take you at least a few weeks to master walking around your bedroom without either falling through the floor or drifting through the ceiling.

Once you are ready to leave your bedroom, just walk through the door. I suggest that you spend the next several astral projection sessions exploring your home. You will be able to see your home in a very different light, and you will also be able to really master the art of navigating your physical body on the physical plane if you take your time to thoroughly explore your home while projecting. Once you are confident that you can navigate throughout your home with your astral body, you can begin exploring your immediate neighborhood in your astral body.

I really suggest that you restrict yourself to working with the physical universe once you master astral projection. You will discover that by thinking of a place you have once been, you can travel there with your astral body almost instantly. This will give you many interesting experiences and insights you will enjoy. Attempting to travel elsewhere, such as visiting the astral realms, may result in a bad trip, so I do not advise it.

Moving Physical Objects with Your Mind

I place this information at this point in my text because the subject is mentioned in this chapter. While it may not seem to be obvious to the casual reader, you must first learn to move objects mentally while you are in your physical body before you begin to move physical objects while you are projecting out of your physical body. This art, known as *telekinesis*, is one which requires both good mental concentration and the exercise of the force of the will. I suggest that you first master the concentration exercises given previously before you attempt to learn this somewhat more difficult art.

There are three classic exercises for mastering telekinesis. I consider them all equally efficient, but my prejudice is with the one which I was first given by my teachers. I will give all three of these exercises here. You will find that once you have success with one of these exercises, you will quickly be able to master the other two without difficulty. You should master all of the exercises before you attempt to use the art while you are projecting out of your body.

The first exercise involves using a piece of thread and a small weight, like a small lead fishline weight. The kind which are similar to split shot work the best. It should only weigh a fraction of an ounce (a gram or so). This weight should be placed on the end of a piece of ordinary sewing thread, with the other end tied to a support so that the weight can swing about an inch or so above a table top.

Now seat yourself on a comfortable chair at the table and focus all your attention on the weight. You must now will the weight to swing to and fro, left to right. You may erect a barrier of paper around the string and weight if you wish to keep any stray drafts from influencing it. Just relax yourself and mentally "will" the weight to swing from one side to the other, without any emotional effort, and without any mental or physical strain.

You may be successful at your first effort, and you may not. But if you keep working at it you will probably find that you will be successful willing the weight to swing within a week or so. The more you are able to concentrate your attention and focus your will on the weight, the more successful you will be.

Once you can will the weight to swing back and forth every time you attempt the exercise for three or four days running, you are ready to go on. You should now tape a piece of paper under the weight and mark the size of the swing you get. You will now increase the size of the swing, from possibly a half inch each side of center to about two-and-a-half inches each side of the rest position. Once you have achieved the greatest possible swing you may go further. Now you must will the weight to swing, and once it is swinging, will the weight to stop. After a few tries you will find that you will be successful at this as well.

The next step is willing the weight to rotate in a circle. Have it rotate clockwise, and then counterclockwise. Lastly, have it rotate clockwise and then stop and return to rest, then swing to and fro, then stop, swing back and forth, and finally rotate counterclockwise. Once you have mastered this exercise you should go on to the other two exercises. Having mastered these three exercises, you may attempt to knock a balanced playing card off your dresser to the floor when you are out of your body. You will find it a bit more difficult, but you will soon be able to accomplish it.

The second classic telekinesis exercise is the one which Elena Petrovna Blavatsky, the founder of the Theosophical Society, used to train her successor, Annie Besant. This involves floating an ordinary sewing needle on the top of a glass full of water, no mean trick in itself for most people today.

With the sewing needle floating on the surface tension of the water, you are to concentrate your attention on the needle and will it to turn in any direction you wish. You should be able to will the needle to turn from pointing at one side to another, and even have it rotate around on the top of the water, moving slowly but steadily. I have seen a woman give readings with such a needle, using the point of the needle to point at letters of the alphabet which were painted on the side of the glass in which the needle floated. Naturally, she controlled the message given by turning the needle, but it is quite impressive to someone who does not either understand or accept that the needle moved under her willed control.

The third exercise involves using a slightly heavier object. This may be made from a Tinkertoy set, or it may be made as I describe it. Take a piece of 1/4 inch dowel rod, about eight inches long. Fix a weight (about an ounce) to each end, and tie it in the center with a string, which will suspend it from any convenient overhead place, as in the exercise involving the lead weight. Again, this may be over a table, or it may be anywhere else you desire. Your task is to will this assembly to rotate, swing back and forth, and generally perform in the same way as you did with the small lead weight.

Once you master this last exercise physically, you should attempt it when you are projecting out of your body. If you can get the assembly to rotate while you are projecting, you will find that you are ready to begin working with small objects while you are out of your body. Begin with knocking balanced playing cards off your dresser, and progress to moving marbles across a table. You may do this by placing a number of marbles in a shallow baking pan and moving them from one side of the pan to the other. While this may not seem like a great achievement on the physical plane, it is quite difficult to do using the mind and "will" alone when you are out of your body. However, once mastered, it will allow you to perform all sorts of small tasks with your will when either in or out of your body.

If you succeed in accomplishing these tasks when you are in your physical body, you will have turned your willpower into a real force in you life. You will have actually developed your willpower into a tool which you can use to your benefit. This, itself, is a worthwhile development.

If you are one of those who can accomplish these tasks when you are projected out of your body, you will find that you are able to accomplish tasks which most people consider to be impossible. Out of your body you may go places on this Earth and do things which interest you. You may read books not otherwise available to you in libraries many miles away from your physical location. You will have mastered the art of projection. Through further work, you will find you will be able to increase your abilities in this very useful art.

Chapter 9
___

ELEMENTAL MAGIC

Elemental magic is a magical practice based on the concept that there are four elements which permeate the material universe. These four elements, and their various combinations, are thought of by magicians as being the basis of all physical creation. These elements are always understood as being forces of the nonphysical universe created by God. These elements were created to be agents through which the physical universe would be made manifest. Elements and elementals are neither Gods nor deities; the elements are simply basic forces or basic "energies" of the nonphysical universe.

When a magician is able to work harmoniously with the four elements it is believed that the elements, or elemental forces, will act favorably at the behest of the magician. Elemental magic may be described as a form of magical practice based upon the ability to communicate with, and direct, rather than control, the four primal elemental forces. Just as working with the dead requires that the magician be able to speak to and hear the dead, so elemental magic requires that the magician be able to communicate with the elemental forces. The magician does this by being in harmony with them. The effort to do so means that there usually must be a particular attitude held toward the divine physical creation on the part of the magician.

These four elements are the nonphysical (often referred to as the spiritual) equivalent of the physical material of Earth, Water, Fire, and Air. The elements are frequently represented by their physical equivalents on many altars. The chalice is the symbol for Water; the patten, or dish, symbolizes Earth; the sword or knife is the symbol for Air; and the light of flame on the altar is the symbol for Fire.

The four symbols found on the four suits of the minor arcanum of the tarot deck are often interpreted as representing the four nonphysical elements. Disks or coins are usually said to represent Earth, cups represent Water, swords represent Air, and slaves (or wands) are said to represent Fire. From there they are compared with the symbols on the ordinary pack of playing cards, where hearts are often said to represent Water, diamonds—Fire, spades—Earth, and clubs—Air. These value assignments, or correspondences, although interesting, have nothing at all to do with either elemental magic or higher occult knowledge.

The mastery of elemental magic is what is intended by the four elemental initiations often found in the practice of ritual and ceremonial magic. These are generally considered to be among the preliminary initiations, usually the third through seventh, which are given in many ceremonial magical lodges. People who have received these elemental initiations may judge for themselves whether or not they have actually mastered this level of spiritual development, by deciding whether or not they can now successfully work magic which produces a physical result through the assistance of the four elements. If people have taken the four elemental initiations in a ceremonial magic group or lodge, and still cannot work with the elements to perform magic, it is a testimony that these individuals have not really earned the initiations which their group has given them.

Some people have a natural affinity for the practice of elemental magic. The work fits them immediately, and they are very successful at it. Just as some people have a natural affinity for working with the dead, some people have a natural affinity for working with elements. There are certain physiological signs that often indicate people who have been born with the natural ability to perform elemental magic. In our present-day society these signs are no guarantee that these people will ever have the chance to learn about, or to perform, any form of magic at all.

One of the physiological indications indicating an ability to work with elemental magic is having pointed ears. These "Dr. Spock" type ears are not very common, but they usually are an indication of people who are able to communicate deeply with nature. Another indication is found in those who have a "green thumb" with plants and other growing things. Having an emotional concern for either wild or domestic animals, or a love for particular pets is not an indication of an uncommon ability to work with the elements.

There are also some indications for an ability to perform elemental magic that may be found in the lines of

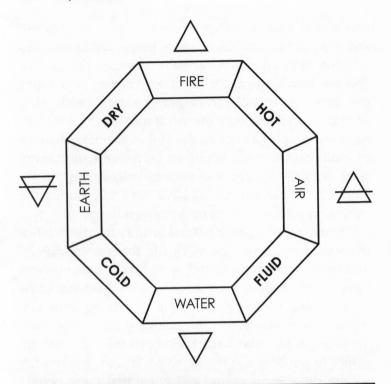

BODY = FEMININE

Water - Feeling = Emotions = Blue = Emotional

Earth - Consciousness of the Ego = Green = Practical

MIND = MASCULINE

Fire - Volition = Will = Mentation = Red = Inspirational

Air - Mental = Intellectual = Communicative = Yellow

Figure 2. The Elements and their qualities. This may be viewed as one form of the octagon.

the palm of the hand. These physiological signs, however, only indicate the potential to develop abilities that will allow work with elemental magic. These individuals must still do the work which will develop themselves to work with the elements. It is usually easier for them than it is for most of us, but it is always hard work.

The theory of the four elements is accepted in most forms of Western magical practice. Those who have some familiarity with Chinese medical or occult thought may remember that the Chinese have a "five element" theory. Hindu metaphysical theory deals with the four European elements. The present Hindu system was adopted from Greek Neoplatonic thought, during the time of the invasion of India by Alexander the Great. It was not a native Aryan concept. The Hindus add "Akasha" or "astral life energy" to the four European elements, as their fifth element, absorbing the concept of five fundamental elements from China. In Western magical practice Akasha, or the Universal Life Force, is not usually considered to be an element. Most European metaphysical schools consider it to be something entirely different.

Because of the widespread acceptance of the four elements by magicians in the West, a lot of the magical work in various practices deals with elemental magic in one form or another. As a magical system, elemental magic is simplicity itself, but it is also very effective. When you review the many rituals of various magical practices, it is often surprising to see just how much of the work involved depends upon the harmonious cooperation of the elements.

The four elements are viewed as the manifesters of creation, and thus they are on the spiritual level next above incarnate human beings. It is usually thought that the elements give a particular "feel" or "vibration" to the various constituents of the physical universe. These elemental energies are understood to be present in all matter, with each of the four elements being present in every particle of matter. Various types of things are said to have various proportions of each element. For example, the physical material we know as Water is said to contain mostly elemental water, containing much less of the other three elements.

Elemental magic also views human characteristics in terms of elements. Emotion is related to elemental water in this system of classification. Sloth would be compared to the elemental force of Earth, while activity would be compared to the elemental force of Fire. Thus emotional spells which are to come to fruition slowly could be worked with Water and Earth.

Elemental magic works with the four elements, either singly or in blends of two or more elements, to accomplish the desires of the magician. A love spell, which is to influence the emotions, would deal with the element of Water, and, as it requires the individual to feel the fire of passion, it would also deal with Fire. To assist its force in being communicated to the intended recipient it might also involve the element Air, which is said to relate to the process of communication. As the magician is only dealing with four elements, it is easy to see that elemental magic is not nearly as complex a system as are most other systems of magic.

When you work directly with elements you are not usually influenced by—or working with—any of the other aspects of the nonphysical world. This makes the practice of elemental magic quite simple. Elemental magic does not require any special physical structure, or any special tools or equipment, as does ritual and ceremonial magic. Neither does elemental magic require a storehouse of herbs and other supplies as does natural magic.

To practice elemental magic, the magician must being by building a harmony with the four elements within. Even in a person with a natural inclination for elemental magic, this can be a very long drawn out affair. It always takes dedication, and self-discipline, as well as time and effort to accomplish. A person with a great natural affinity with a particular element will need at least six months effort to begin to harmonize with the element.

You must bring yourself into harmony with any element before you begin working with it. This means that the elemental forces must accept you. Your acceptance of them is taken for granted. Once harmony with one element is mastered, it is necessary to being developing harmony with the others. This requires persistence and discipline until inner harmony with all four elements is obtained. The whole process of harmonization with the elements takes at least four years of hard, disciplined work. It is a sufficiently difficult process to discourage anyone who is not serious about attaining this goal.

Achieving harmony with the elements is the most difficult part of learning to perform elemental magic. Once the potential magician achieves harmony with the elements, the actual performance of elemental magic is simplicity itself. The elements are simply respectfully spoken with, and asked to assist the magician to achieve the goals the magician is seeking. Sometimes physical symbols of the elements are used to give the prayer a focus, or to assist in bringing the results of the magician's prayer to physical manifestation more quickly.

In Hindu prayer, or puja, colored powders are often blown to the four cardinal directions. This may be thought of as a form of elemental magic, in that it is actually an offering to the elements of Earth and Air to accomplish a task. This is one example of the application of elemental magic in a magico-religious practice. There are many more which could be cited. In the case of puja, the colors of the powders used may correspond to the deities being invoked. The powders being blown into the air are thought to assist in carrying the prayer to the deity.

In a strictly magical practice, working with the elements, candles, and flash paper may be used to aid the magician in working with fire elementals, while dissolving rice paper may be used to assist in prayers to water elementals. Prayers can also be made at a running brook or river to influence the water elementals on one's behalf. Incense or blown powders can be used in prayers to air elementals. Loam, clay, or potting soil can be used to gain the aid of earth elementals. The well known graveyard dirt, so famous in folklore and voodoo spells, is actually a focus for payer to earth elementals. Graveyard dirt is just dirt taken from a fresh grave.

While the elementals are actually nonphysical forces, they are anthropomorphized by magicians and metaphysicians just like everything else that human beings encounter. Thus you will find references to the "King of the Earth Elementals" and "Grand Duke of the Water Spirits" and so forth in some magical literature.

Gnomes are supposedly representatives of earth elementals. Mermaids are often viewed in Western magical practices as water elementals who live in the ocean. Undines are supposedly the lovely water elementals that live in fresh water. Salamanders are supposedly creatures of the fire elementals. Sylphs, understood to be lovely transparent female forms, are the personification or anthropomorphization of air elementals.

Some magico-religious practices credit these "little people" with being elementals, while others do not. In the Afro-Cuban Santeria practice, for example, mermaids are not usually thought of as water elementals, they are usually thought of as being separate spiritual entities. Some English speaking ceremonialists would actively disagree with this viewpoint. This is just another example of the diversity of views held by the various magical practices.

Once you contact the elemental forces by harmonizing with them, it is not necessary to anthropomorphize them. You are quite aware that they are real, and that they are not anything of what you might have been led to expect, no matter how extensive your reading and intellectual study of the subject.

Chapter 10

LEARNING ELEMENTAL MAGIC

Elemental magic, as was previously mentioned, depends a great deal on your having a natural faculty. You should first determine that you have a faculty to practice elemental magic, if you do not, forget the idea unless you have a teacher who is guiding you in that direction. If you do not have a teacher, you should work with the concentration and meditation exercises listed in the books mentioned in chapter 5. These exercises will get your mind to the point it has to be to use it as a tool to work with the elements. These exercises, especially the concentration exercises, are basic to any practice of magic, and to astral projection as well. Once you have mastered them you can go on to work with the elements.

Begin by growing plants—even a few plants in a window box. Grow them with love and pay close attention to them, concentrating on them as you tend them. Talk to them, and work with them in a fully focused way. When you have really mastered this art you will find that the plants will wordlessly "talk" back to you. Continue to develop friendship and communication with your plants. Within a short time you will find that you have opened the way to understanding the kingdom (or realm) of the earth elementals.

Developing this communication will take several years if you have the faculty. If you do not have the faculty, it will bring you closer to developing it, so any time you spend attempting this work is not going to be wasted. Do not be impatient with this exercise, as impatience will make it more difficult to master. Simply keep working at it without expecting anything, eventually you will start communicating with the plants.

Once you open communication with the earth elementals you will find that communication with other elementals will open progressively in time. Just keep working with your plants and focusing on them to the exclusion of any extraneous things while you are working with them. You don't have to "love" them, you just have to respect the plants and tend them.

To perform magic with the plants you should just mention to the elements what you need while you are working with them. The only caveats are that you have to be able to really communicate with them, and you have to know what you really need.

Understanding the elements may be accomplished by reading some of the following material and thinking about it. Nothing that you can read will allow you to gain a real acquaintance with the elements, this must be gained by actually being introduced to them on a non-physical level. I mention a number of ways of looking at the elements below. There are many ways of looking at them, but none of these ways is like meeting them.

Fire is the principal of activity.

Water is the principal of attraction.

Air is the principal of communication, or inter-action.

Earth is the principal of stability, or inertia.

These principals can be expressed in a manner similar to the binary logic of a computer.

Fire with Air to Water equals 1 in binary logic.

Fire with Earth to Water equals 0 in binary logic.

From this viewpoint, Earth as the intermediary prevents communication, and forms an "open circuit," while Air, when it replaces Earth, forms a "closed circuit."

Fire and Water are said to be the primordial elements. The spiritual forces of the universe are said to have been created from Fire, while the physical forces of the universe, including mankind, are said to have been created from Water.

The Star of David, the symbol of Judaism, may be viewed as the Fire and Water principal in perfect balance. The equilateral triangle with the point upward is said to be a symbol of Fire while the same triangle with the point downward is said to be a symbol of Water.

Plato considered Earth and Fire the fundamental elemental forces. He said that Fire had the qualities of brightness, thinness and motion. He said that Earth had the qualities of darkness, thickness and quietness. Plato said that there were two Airs, and two Waters. The Air of Fire had the quality of thinness and motion, while the Air of Earth had the quality of darkness. The Water of Fire had the quality of motion, and the Water of Earth the qualities of thickness and darkness.

Agrippa said that Fire was hot and dry. He added that Earth was dry and cold, Water was cold and moist, and Air was moist and hot. He considered Earth and Water to be passive and feminine, while Fire and Air he considered to be active and masculine.

Fire and Air are said to be a part of the formless universe, while Earth and Air are said to be a part of the formative universe.

If you meditate upon one of these statements at a time, after you have thought about it consciously, you may gain some insight into the way the elements manifest in the physical world. This will assist in developing the ability to harmonize yourself with the elements.

Chapter 11

NATURAL MAGIC

When we study the systems and practices of magic we are dealing with operations of magic as it is thought out by the mind. Beneath our belief structure and intellectual expression, exists a foundation upon which the operations of all magic actually rests. This foundation holds faithful and true despite beliefs or intellectual rationalizations. The basis for magic is as true as the proven laws of physics, and like these physical laws, it does not require recognition or acceptance by human intelligence for its operation. It does require that the humans using these laws possess certain faculties. It is the possession of these non-physical faculties that allows people to be magicians.

Working with spirits of the dead, whether to obtain information or to perform magic, depends less on beliefs, and more on one's faculty for the work, than either religious magic or ritual and ceremonial magic. Elemental magic may be decorated with beliefs of various kinds, anthropomorphizations of the elemental forces and other unnecessary complications. The real practice of elemental magic, however, is entirely dependent upon the ability of magicians to place themselves in harmony with the elemental forces of the universe. The ability to achieve harmonization with the elemental forces is entirely a human faculty.

In this respect, natural magic is of the same nature. The practice of magic through the use of natural materials such as stones, plants, animals, earth and other naturally occurring things depends almost entirely upon the individual's ability to really harmonize with these materials and learn why the Creator has provided them for the use of humanity. In natural magic, ingredients used are selected for their relevance to the desires of the magician. They are then prayed over by the magician, to give them direction. You could say that they are instructed by the magician in prayer to exert their natural influence in the manner that the magician desires. Just as with the practice of elemental magic, and the practice of working with spirits of the dead, natural magic requires that the magician develop various non-physical faculties so that his or her magical ability can operate.

Natural magic depends for its effects on the inherent power or virtue of the natural ingredients used, and it depends on its direction for the prayer of the magician. Natural magic is entirely different from magical systems that depend on beliefs. The ingredients used in a spell are not concerned with what is in the mind of the magician when he or she prays over them. It is the magician's ability to pray which causes the ingredients of the spell to respond as he or she desires.

The natural ingredients of a magical spell are not concerned with whether the magician is doing "good" or "evil." The concern of these ingredients is only that they have been applied for use in the manner in which they were intended by the creator of the universe. Natural magic is very effective. It is so effective that it forms a part of almost all other practices of magic.

When natural magic is used in conjunction with other, more intellectual, systems of magic, the various parts of the physical universe which are used as ingredients in the practice are usually identified with deities, forces of the universe, emanations of God, and so forth. Plants, flowers, herbs, incenses, perfumes and so forth are all allocated relevant spaces in the framework of the intellectually-oriented magical practice. An example of this intellectual categorization is the well-known book, *777 & Other Qabalistic Writings*, by Aleister Crowley. It is a guide to those who work with the Christianized Cabbala according to his system. In truth, the attributes of these natural objects depend on their actual inherent virtue, or natural active power. The power of these natural objects is inherent to them, and exists as a part of their essential being. The essential power is only enlivened by the prayer of the person who works with them.

The mythology of any magical or religious system must be structured to account for the fundamental virtue of the natural materials used in its work. This usually requires that the virtues or the active power of the natural materials be explained in terms of the mythologies of the system. It also means that the actual virtue of the material is usually modified, at least a bit, to conform to the intellectual mythology of the system.

Natural magic may be used either with or without a belief structure or any explanation of why it works. In the hands of those who can pray, it becomes a true technology, as people can successfully perform any spell for which they can locate the proper ingredients. It is this gradual development of traditional spells, which use the virtues of stones, plants, and animals, that forms the basis for almost all systems of folk magic.

What is required in those who would be practitioners of natural magic is the subtle ability to see or sense the interconnection between the material at hand and the magic goals they have set for themselves. This requires an ability to perceive the real nature of things, an ability beyond the reach of the bulk of humanity. This faculty is the subtle perception of reality which has been mentioned by mystics of all creeds. It is the true understanding which comprehends that the creation is the ultimate work of one force, and that all of the variations in creation are simply facets of this one divine being.

Robert Fludd and Paracelsus both mentioned this perception in relation to magic, as have many other mystics. Some esoteric texts set about to train inquirers to develop this perception, usually with very indifferent results. All that may really be said about it is that it is a faculty, a talent, which is not shared uniformly by humankind. There have been enough of those who have had this ability, however, to have left a large body of traditional spells, which can be used very effectively by those who have the ability to pray.

Many of the spells of natural magic are published in inexpensive spell books available in lower income areas of larger cities. These spells are used every day by people who wish to gain advantage for themselves in their daily contact with the world. Fritz Leiber's famous book *Conjur Wife* is a novel based upon the pervasion of natural magical techniques in our everyday society, at a very hidden level. It is at this hidden, but all-pervasive level of society that natural magic constantly operates. It is in constant use in our society, and in all other societies.

In addition to the authentic spell books, there are many "nonsense works" available. Many have been written only to make money for those who sell "occult" materials. Others contain spells which have had excess ingredients added, by writers who have found that the original spells do not work in their hands. Merchants have added superfluous ingredients, or mysterious potions, to spells to confuse the issue or to increase profit. Yet many real natural magic spells exist, and are used by hundreds of people.

The prayer over the ingredients, which activates and directs them, is another source of difficulty. Despite the real ease of prayer, many people cannot send a prayer further than their voices. The inability of most people to pray successfully is frequently taken as a failure of natural magic. Those who cannot pray either add ingredients to a spell to "make it work" or decide that natural magic doesn't work.

In the 18th century a plant known as *Lobellia Syphletica*, or Blue Lobelia, was used as a cure for syphilis. It had a rather spotty reputation, and in the mid-19th century it was practically dropped from the herbal repertory. At the present time it is used only by folk healers for the treatment of this disease. The problem was not with the plant, but with the physicians. Physicians in the 18th century learned of the plant, and of its use, from folk healers. The folk healers carefully picked the flowers and dried them for later use. Then, when applying the flowers, in the form of a decoction, as a treatment, the folk healers sincerely prayed over them. Their prayer activated the flowers of the plant, and made it a curative agent. Without the prayer there was little, if any, medical benefit found in the plant. Today the medical profession has better and faster working treatments for almost every condition and no longer work with basic herbal remedies. However the herbal remedies are still there for those who can use them.

There are a number of other cases which may be cited in this regard. The tincture of Muira Puama root is said to cure male impotency. It works well if it is prayed over, but I understand that it has little or no effect as a medicine by itself. The same is true of many perfumes and incenses. The quality of many incense ingredients is changed if they are prayed over before being burned. Myrrh, when it is used in summoning spirits to a visible appearance, is only one example, but it is a dramatic one.

Prayer is an essential in any kind of magic, as it is an essential in life itself. The general inability of people to pray successfully is a great lack in our modern society. You can not hope to be a complete human being until you are able to offer a sincere prayer of thanks to your creator for the opportunity which has been offered you by the life you are now enjoying. If you find that you cannot pray, your first task in life is to learn to pray.

There is no real way to teach people how to pray, except on a one to one basis over a period of time. One of the great saints of Islam was once criticized for discouraging some of his students from praying the Islamic ritual prayers. He replied to the effect that it was better if they first learned how to pray, before they blocked themselves from the possibility of learning, by pretending that they could pray.

There are exercises to assist most people in gradually developing the ability to pray. One of the best is to repeat a "set prayer" constantly throughout the day. Roman Catholics might use the Hail Mary, or the Our Father. Jews can use the Schma (Hear Oh Israel, The Lord, The Lord thy God is One!). Eventually this simple exercise will bear fruit, although it must be done regularly for years before there is even a tremor indicating that any real growth has taken place. Eventually, the growth will happen. Once a person has developed to a sufficiently elevated spiritual place, it is possible to perform natural magic. Until that time the person cannot perform Natural Magic.

Chapter 12

LEARNING NATURAL MAGIC

In order to understand natural magic we need to learn how to recognize natural virtues. Aside from using the "psychic senses," there are ways in which natural objects announce the vital power of their virtue to the physical senses. There are some obvious rules for determining the natural virtue of things, but as we shall see, there can be no physical or intellectual replacement for the interior sight used to find the true connections between the things of this world.

Natural magic is the application of the force of natural objects to assist the astral force of an incarnate human being to promote a change in the physical world.

The intellectual discernment of the natural virtue of things, often referred to as their rulership, is the well-known "doctrine of signatures." This doctrine is based upon the belief that the Creator of all things put a "signature" upon every created thing. The principal is that the "signature" or identification of the virtue is based upon the physical appearance of the natural object. This gives us our first rule for determining the virtue of things from the doctrine of signatures:

> All natural things display their virtue by their physical shape, form and color.

The great physician and occultist Paracelsus "developed the doctrine of signatures which he had inherited from Albertus Magnus, and which was reinforced by his own acute observations and use of herbal remedies. This theory is based on the idea that every part of man, the microcosmic world, corresponds to some part of the universe, the macrocosmic world, and that the connection will be obvious by some similarity of form or color, in fact by its Signature."[1]

In accordance with the doctrine of signatures, we find that those plants which have leaves shaped like a lance or a blade have the signature (astrologically) of Mars, and are often beneficial in the treatment of wounds. Many of these herbs are called Vulneraries to this day, as they have been used for this purpose in the past.

By the same token, plants which have red leaves, or red flowers, have the same signature, and also are said to have the virtue of those things astrologically equated

---

[1]Stephen Skinner, from the introduction to *The Archidoxes of Magic* by Paracelsus (New York: Samuel Weiser, 1975), p. ii.

with Mars. The virtues of the planets are the "exterior virtues," in that the planets are visible in the skies. The virtues of the plants are the "interior virtues," in that they are concealed in the plants and must be released by prayer.

In the middle ages this doctrine of signatures was accepted in many places, and in some of the older herbals, many of the plants were identified with a planet. Sometimes this was also carried over into the formal medical practice, with the plant being listed as "suitable for diseases of Mars," or with some similar statement. Unfortunately, many of the physicians of the time could not pray, and thus they could not fully activate the plants or herbal medicines they used to treat diseases.

Plants which have a quantity of water with their leaves, or which have white flowers or whitish leaves, are related to the Moon by their signature. They may be useful in treating diseases of the periodic function, or in treating the diseases of women. These plants are certainly useful in the practice of magic, as magic is related to those things astrologically ruled by the Moon.

We have seen how the virtues of the planets are related to the virtues of plants. This relationship is usually limited to the seven "visible" planets, known since antiquity. These "ancient seven" are said to exert the strongest influence on the individual nativity (horoscope), and daily influence the individual in life on Earth.

In the system of astrological rulerships, there are other rulerships used as well. The twelve signs of the zodiac are said to rule particular plants, and the more recently discovered planets—Uranus, Neptune, and Pluto—have also had plant rulerships assigned to them. This yields a total of twenty-two influences assigned in the astrological system of rulership. In addition, plants are also said, along with other natural materials, to have particular correspondence with the four elements: Earth, Air, Fire, and Water.

Following the astrological or any other system of rulership or attribution that one might use, the real "virtues" of plants, animals, and so on, becomes quite blended. It is possible to have a great deal of difficulty in identifying the fundamental virtue of any natural thing through the use of any set of reference beliefs. It is always better to refer to the "interior sight" in determining connections, as was mentioned previously by Paracelsus.

By referring to the "interior sight" I am referring to that part of the human awareness most difficult to develop. If you wish to sense whether you may have this ability, you can try an experiment. Simply hold a sample of any natural material, such as a leaf, in your hand. Now project your consciousness into the material. Once you blend yourself with the material, it is only necessary to ask, "What are you?" The material, itself, will answer the question, and you will know. In this interchange there will be no use of words or language.

This is about the best description possible of what is entirely a nonverbal form of communication. If words, rational thoughts or any other interchanges are present in addition to the transfer to knowledge from one consciousness to the other, it is not "interior sight."

In attempting this practice of "interior sight" it is best to avoid deceiving yourself that you have an answer when you do not. Should this trial be attempted and there is no answer, it is best to admit it at once and avoid any form of self-deception.

I have been using the term "virtue" in a particular way here. The term is almost interchangeable with the term "vibrations" as used by the "new age conscious-ness" people, or by those who practice holistic healing. Virtue is the specific quality of anything which is a part of the divine creation. So that you do not confuse the "virtue" of a thing with the "vibrations" of a thing, the way it feels when it is held, let me define as accurately as possible just what it means when I say "virtue."

> Virtue is the merit or good quality of some part of the divine creation. It is an effective and active force in the physical world—it has the power to produce a particular effect. Virtue is inherent within the natural material or object, and not placed there from without as the result of any form of processing or treatment, includ-ing prayer.

If you think about this definition, you will find that everything has a virtue. The virtue must first be identi-fied, and then it may be applied. The virtue of some-thing as complex as a plant, for example, is not constant throughout its entire growth. The virtue is modified depending upon what part of the natural object, say a plant, the sample is taken.

As an example of the way in which the older herbals treated the virtues of plants, by listing their governance and virtues, the following notes are taken from a reprint of the classic *Culpeper's Herbal*.

> Agrimony—Moderately hot and moist accord-ing to the nature of Jupiter.

Aloe—It is a martial plant, hot in the second degree, and dry in the third; of a very bitter taste.

Azalea—It is a plant of Mercury, and has a pleasing aromatic smell.

Bramble (Blackberry)—It is a plant of Venus in Aries.

Willow—The Moon owns it.[2]

While not all of the plants mentioned are treated in this way, many of them have detailed listings of their rulership and virtues. These may be put to good use by anyone interested in either herbal healing or natural magic.

A plant (or an animal) has a number of constituent parts. The roots, stem, bark, leaves, flowers and seeds of a plant all have different subrulerships according to the doctrine of signatures.(See figure 3 on page 129.) If we are working with a plant, we must consider the part of the plant we are working with when we consider its virtue. If we are using "interior sight," this difference will come to us automatically. If we are relying on any system of rulership classification, astrological or otherwise, we will find that we have entered into a very complex system indeed.

Referring back to the system of astrological rulerships, the parts of the plant which are underground have as their subruler the influence of Saturn. The vir-

[2]In *Culpeper's Complete Herbal and English Physician*, pp. 1, 8, 13, 23, and 199. There are many reprints available of this classic text, such as the 1987 edition published by Meyerbooks of Glenwood, Illinois.

tue of Saturn will permeate the root system of any plant. The bark of the root is the communication with the external world of the root, and therefore has a sub-rulership of Mercury. We might say that the bark of the root of the plant is ruled by the virtue of Mercury cojoined with Saturn. This applies to the bark of the root of any plant.

The fruit of the plant is ruled by Jupiter. In the case of the potato, the fruit is underground. Now the potato itself is ruled by Venus, and the fruit of the potato is the Venus-ruled Jupiter of Saturn. Venus rules the potato plant altogether, Jupiter rules the fruit of the plant, the potato itself, which has a subrulership of Saturn, because it is grown underground.

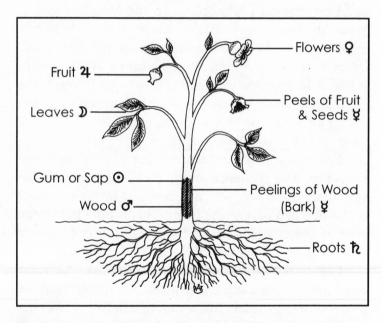

Figure 3. Astrological rulership of plants according to Paracelsus. (Illustration courtesy Alden Cole.)

In the same astrological system, carrots are ruled by Mercury. The carrot is the fruit of the plant, so it has the virtue of Jupiter, while the growth of the carrot takes place underground, so the virtue of Saturn is added. Thus the carrot can be referred to as the Mercury-ruled Jupiter of Saturn.

Obviously, the peelings of both the carrot and the potato, being the skins of the roots, have in addition the influence of Mercury. From this observation it should be easy to see that potato peelings can be used to keep a lover faithful, while carrot peelings can open opportunities for business income. In fact, both carrots and potatoes can be used in this way in the practice of natural magic!

This system of astrological rulerships was developed by magical philosophers in the Middle Ages. It grows to great complexity, which we have only briefly indicated here. While it does have some practical application, I do not recommend going into it at any depth. While it is possible to make connections through the astrological rulership of the plants themselves, it becomes an awesome task to do so correctly. How much easier it is to use interior sight!

The fundamental influence of any plant is the major influence. The influence of any part of the plant is the secondary influence, which is modified by the influence of the detailed part of the plant. This is only the beginning of the complexities of the classification of nature according to any system of intellectual rulership.

Color, taste, and scent are three qualities which also enter into determining the virtue of a plant through the doctrine of signatures. In the case of a radish, which has the basic influence of Mars, the radish is more strongly connected with Mars if it is red on its outside (Mars =

red). A white radish has a sub-influence of the Moon, and therefore relates to the Jupiter (fruit) with Saturn (underground) modification of the Mercury influence, with a lesser influence of the Moon! You can see how complex this problem of rulerships becomes.

We have seen that the process of assigning influences and virtues through any system of intellectual rulerships is quite complex. The astrological system is no more complex than any other system based on deific rulerships, emanations, paths, or whatever. While I have only touched on the complexities of the astrological system of classification, I will mention briefly that the time and manner of picking certain plants has an additional influence on the "virtues" of the plant.

The astrological system of rulerships is an easy system to explore, as during the Middle Ages debates were held on the subject by many academic authorities. Many of these debates have been recorded and can be consulted by interested investigators in the libraries of Europe. Some of the magical classics have recently been reprinted. What constitutes a "scientific paper" in one era is likely to be seen very differently a few hundred years later.

The process of identifying the virtue of a plant or other natural object is obviously much easier when you use your faculty of "interior sight." This faculty is the same as the faculty of "intuitive understanding" occasionally mentioned by other writers of occult lore. It is a spiritual sense or faculty, not one that may be learned through the exercise or training of the rational mental processes. On the other hand, the process of determining the virtue of things through correspondences, astrological or otherwise, is an intellectual process, and requires the exercise and training of the mental process.

In this case, using the rational mental faculty to determine virtues is really going the long way around something to learn only a part of what is obvious to the person with interior sight.

The faculty of intuitive insight, used to sense the virtue of things, is learned by studying with teachers who have also developed that faculty. It can be learned in no other way. Exercises are required to open the process, and then other exercises are required to make certain that students have a balanced development. The exercises may seem to have little to do with anything the students wish to learn, and most students lose faith and drop out of the training. This is probably a necessary part of the training, for only strongly committed students can develop the ability. Those who either have this ability or who develop it will probably go on to learn the intricacies of the processes of magic.

Some Rules
of Natural Magic

The identification of the virtues of natural things is a complex process when done through the use of the intellectual faculty. It seems simple when done through the use of the "interior sight" or inner knowledge. Until we can view things from the standpoint of inner knowledge it is impossible to understand how simple natural magic is.

How is it that prayer is able to motivate the forces of natural things to act in accordance with the human will?

There are laws in the realm of natural magic, just as there are laws in the realm of intellectual thought. I mentioned the doctrine of signatures earlier. The action of human prayer on natural things is in accordance with another rule, the "law of dominion."

The inferior is subject to the superior.

In the Christian, Hebrew, and Islamic canonical writings, the Bible and Koran, this rule of dominion is expressed. In the Bible it is stated in the Eighth Psalm, verses four through eight. The psalm is a clear statement of the control over the natural forces of the universe that the creator of the universe has blessed us with if we can only recognize and understand it.

Psalm 8

4 What is man, that thou art mindful of him? and the son of man, that thou visitest him?

5 For thou hast made him a little lower than the angels, and hast crowned him with glory and honour.

6 Thou madest him to have dominion over the works of thy hands; thou hast put all things under his feet:

7 All sheep and oxen, yea, and the beasts of the field;

8 The fowl of the air, and the fish of the sea, and whatsoever passeth through the paths of the seas.

It is the actual demonstrable fact of this dominion, not the belief that they have dominion, which gives the right to work natural magic in the eyes of the Creator. Those who are able to demonstrate this dominion are the true priests and priestesses of God upon Earth. For their Father in Heaven has given unto them the true deputyship of creation. They are the real shepherds of His flock. Unto them is given the real authority and the power—a power often claimed by those upstarts and bigots who usually rant against them.

The prayer of the incarnate human being activates the natural material and is neither a demand nor a compulsion directed at or to the material being prayed over. It is the action of the transmission of power from the astral force of the incarnate human being to the spirit of the natural material. This transfer of power encourages the natural material to fulfill its function by "activating" or awakening the material. The material is said to have been "vivified" or "awakened to life" after it has been prayed over. From the level of perception of those who are able to see such things, it might be said to have been changed in some way through the action of prayer.

Prayer is a real force in the universe. Prayer is. Those who are really able to pray have an ability of value, not only to themselves, but to the whole world. People who are not able to pray in this manner should pray anyway. It is only through the action of prayer that we learn the true secret of prayer. The sincere desire to learn how to pray is the key to learning to pray successfully.

There is another rule which applies to the process of directing natural materials to a magical goal. This rule might seem the opposite of the former rule, but it is not; in fact, it is complementary. It will require a bit of objective thought to understand just how this rule operates. Our society views submission in a negative way, and when the term is used, there is usually an internal negative emotional reaction to the word which blots out an understanding of just what submission actually means.

Before we can grow spiritually, we must first submit ourselves to the will of the Creator. In Islam, this submission is the very name of the religion, as the Arabic word *Islam* means submission. Our "humanness" in the world constantly acts in terms of surface interests, rather than in terms of our eternal spiritual interest. The silence of the still, small voice within us is overwhelming, because we have seldom listened to it. Until we turn away from our material interests and submit ourselves, as a spirit, to the will of the Creator, it will be impossible to make any real progress in our spiritual lives. With this in mind we are ready to consider the complement of the rule of dominion.

That which submits rules.

In natural magic, when an incarnate human being prays over the natural material being activated, the natural material gains a direction and a purpose. The natural material submits itself to the will of the person making the prayer. Through its submission, it gains a rulership, in that it now rules the performance of the magical goal set for it by the person who offered the prayer. From this submission, it participates in an interchange of energy, acquiring power from the incarnate human being.

This law is known as the "law of submission," and it is in accordance with the law of submission that work is accomplished in the practice of natural magic. We cannot give true submission to a task that is impossible for us, and thus the material chosen for the particular magical work must be able to accomplish the work for which it is chosen. Identification of the proper material to be used to obtain the desired result is the first step in any action of natural magic.

The virtues of the natural materials used must be harmonious with the magical work performed. If the material you select has a virtue discordant with the work you desire it will not work. For example, some of the spells that appear in popular spell books recommend the addition of ingredients that actually hinder the work that the spell is supposed to accomplish. We can only surmise that these spells were written by people who didn't understand how to work with natural magic spells.

Once you know that you can pray, the next step is to attempt some simple spells with natural ingredients. If the spell does not work, ask each of the materials in turn if it can work in the spell. Occasionally you are able to make your first contact with the natural ingredients by this method because you have some personal involvement with what you are doing. You should expand the contact before you do any further spells, however. The "interior vision" makes all things possible; spells become a much more secondary issue once interior vision is developed.

There is another rule of Natural Magic which must be introduced at this point. This rule is often called the

"Rule of Persistence." It is based upon the idea that the divine creation, as made by God, is perfect, and that this perfection is eternal. Persistence is the primary attribute of the true magician, the drive for this persistence is maintained with the will power of each magician.

Will power, when applied to the desired goal of magic, is the primary power that directs the astral nature of the magician, whether in prayer or in any other endeavor in life. Originating in the mental sphere, as a part of the process of mentation, will power is what gives direction to the magic or the prayer. The rational decision of the magician to engage in a particular act of magic is also important. This decision is the subject of the willed command to the astral nature of the magician to manifest the result the magician desires.

The magician must be able to "will" with unending force, once his or her decision is made, so that what is wished for is in fact made manifest in the physical world. The magician looks for a state of perfection. The magician wills this perfection into being, and manifests it in the world. And thus it is, and shall remain for its allotted time, perfect in the eyes of the one who decreed it and called it forth.

Perfection is eternal.

When you have directed a material or natural object to perform in a certain way, it will continue to direct its efforts and energies as it has been commanded until it is commanded to stop, or until it has completed its task. The direction of the material, coming from its being brought to life by the prayer of the magician, is from the very core of its being. No matter how finely divided the substance is, it will continue to exert its influence under the will of the person who prayed it to life, even throughout all eternity.

We might expect that the death of the person who had such a strong effect on the material through prayer would release the material from attempting to fulfill its assigned task. This is only partially so. The death of the person will only disconnect the living vital energy from the material or object. It will not put an end to the attempt to fulfill that which it was called into being to do. The death of the magician does not end the spell.

One of the most important facts of all magical operations is the necessity of placing a time limit on them. The natural material worked with, or prayed over, must be restricted in time in its operation. If this is not done, the person who has practiced Natural Magic successfully will spend a great deal of time after physical death attempting to bring a halt to those operations which were engendered while the person was alive. This unpleasant consequence may be avoided by remembering to place a time limit upon any spell or work of magic which is to be done, regardless of the purpose.

There are various ways to limit spells in time. One of the easiest ways is to require that a particular effect be achieved, the achieving of the effect to end the work. For example, in a prayer the person might say, "To protect N.N. against any negative influence until her child is born." Or, "To reduce the swelling and the pain until the arm is healed." These accurate statements of what is to be done will also act to limit the operation of the spell in time. One can also say "for six months" to put a definite date on the effects desired.

In a civil wedding ceremony the limit of time is set, "Until death do you part." This is also a limitation of time, and many spells can be timed in this manner. The most important point is to limit all spells in time.

There are various magical systems, and most of them have conflicting viewpoints regarding the number of times a prayer needs to be intoned in order to complete a spell. My own teacher was taught that prayers needed to be repeated seven times, but in his personal experience he learned that a prayer only needed to be said once. He suggested that I could use my intuition in the matter. You will find that various schools of thought offer specific rules and you, too, will have to make up your own mind as to what works for you.

The foregoing will explain why there are three or more versions of the rule that follows. While each version is different, they all come out to the same thing in the end. You should make the prayer as frequently as you feel that it is necessary to do so.

The Rule of Three: Thrice spoken, once fulfilled.

This rule is based upon the concept that a thing said three times will be made manifest. In many Christian magical practices, prayers are made three times, once for each member of the Trinity.

The Rule of Seven: Say a thing seven times and it shall be true.

This rule is apparently based on the concept that a prayer should be said once for each of the seven planetary forces of antiquity. I have also seen this rule stated as, "Say a thing seven times and all who hear it spoken will believe it." In some ancient religious practices prayers were said to the four directions, up to the heavens and down to the earth. The last saying of the prayer was inward, being projected from the nape of the neck. This gives seven repetitions of the prayer.

> The Rule of Nine: Make a prayer nine times and
> God will answer it.

The rule of nine is apparently based on the idea that there are nine major forces which participate in each of the repetitions of the prayer, sending it to the Creator on the last repetition. This rule was explained to me as the reason for the novena (a series of nine prayers) in the Roman Catholic Church.

• • •

The above rules give you a great number of choices in the number of times you pray over something to bring it to life. Some published spells have their own number of repetitions, which should be followed. In other cases, you can use your own feelings in the matter.

Should the question of the human voice having the ability to bring a change in the material world be brought up in the mind of the student, we might append the words of one of the great Indian spiritual teachers, one who opposed the practice of magic as participating in the world of illusion.

> Man's word is Spirit in man. Spoken words are
> sounds occasioned by the vibrations of thoughts;
> thoughts are vibrations sent forth by the ego of
> the soul. Every word you utter should be potent
> with soul vibration. A man's words are lifeless if

he fails to impregnate them with spiritual force. Talkativeness, exaggeration, or falsehood makes your words as ineffective as paper bullets shot from a toy gun. The speech and prayers of garru-lous or inaccurate persons are unlikely to pro-duce beneficial changes in the order of things. Man's words should represent not only truth but also his definite understanding and realization. Speech without soul force is like husks without corn.[3]

This statement by Paramahansa Yogananda is the most accurate statement of what is required to make a true prayer that I have ever read. By impregnating our words with the very force of our soul, we are able to literally work wonders in our daily life. This state of speech is to be desired if we are to practice any mode of magic.

• • •

The next rule is based upon the concept that the physi-cal world (including human beings) was created from water, while the world of the spirit, the astral realms, were created from fire. Fire and Water are said to be the primordial elements, and the following rule shows that the nature of magic is an operation that deals with the astral, or fiery nature of things. Because the spiritual and astral realms are superior to the physical nature, through the law of dominion, the physical nature must

---

[3]Paramahansa Yogananda, *Scientific Healing Affirmations* (Los Angeles: Self-Realization Fellowship, 1981), p. 3.

submit to the astral nature. Thus the physical nature rules in the physical creation, subject only to the astral will.

One who manipulates the fiery astral nature of things will then be able to manipulate the physical universe through understanding of the astral universe. A magician manipulates the powerful forces of the universe only through knowledge, and always with an attitude of respect toward them.

Fire permeates all.

One of the corollaries of this rule is that often the first element the novice magician learns to manipulate is the element fire. Teachers build the relationship between the element fire and the student because the student's acquaintance with natural physical fire leads to becoming acquainted indirectly with the spiritual element fire. Once this acquaintance is established, the magician gains the knowledge of the other elements, one at a time. Teachers usually select the elements closest to the student.

When a person is making the acquaintance of the elements without the guidance of a teacher, it is far safer to begin with the most stable element, earth. In this way the elements will present themselves to the student as the student develops.

There are some further rules of magical operations, most of which are not exclusively used in natural magic. These rules are used in a variety of magical practices. A thorough understanding of these rules will make any magician's lot a bit easier.

The Law of Sympathy: Like produces like.

According to the law of sympathy, if one takes an object which is a symbol of something, and treats it in a certain way, that which the object is a symbol of will respond in the same manner. The most familiar example of this is probably the "doll" or "poppet" so often referred to in stories of the occult. A doll, which is a symbol of a person, is made, often dressed like the person. The doll is treated as the magician wishes the person treated, and the person symbolized by the doll will, in theory, suffer the effect placed on the doll by the magician. This type of magic is a great favorite in love spells.

Many occult and curio shops sell candles shaped like men or women which are burned a bit at a time to cause the victim to "burn with passion" for the one who casts the spell. This idea of sympathy is also used for healing, with prayers for recovery being made over a doll, or the doll being covered with healing herbs. Dolls made from the subject's cast off clothing are a favorite symbol among many magicians.

Other symbols of the person may be used, such as articles of clothing or even photographs, sketches and drawings of him or her. Over the last twenty years, the use of Polaroid photographs for making symbols of people receiving magical healing work has grown quite extensive. These photos certainly make a better symbol than a rough sketch.

Stemming from the law of sympathy is the law of contagion. This law reveals that when two things are in contact, there remains an invisible astral bond between them. This astral bond (or thread) may be used so that an action taken on one thing produces an effect on the other, to which it was formerly connected in some way.

One of the esoteric reasons why monogamy is stressed by the higher members of the spiritual hierarchy is that it limits connections with others. The strongest astral connection one human being can make with another is the sexual bond. This sexual bond may be utilized in many ways by a magician, but at the higher levels it is a source of drain on the magician, who by this time has made spiritual connections with a large number of people, and is not looking for any more.

According to one theory, when you have a sexual connection with another person in life, this connection continues as a spiritual link after death. It is this network of spiritual connections which were formed physically, life after life, which, according to this theory, holds humanity together.

In some practices the thread or connection between people and things is taken quite seriously. For example, a whole set of dogma exists in Hindu magical practice as to which kind of tie is best for which kind of magic. In the Kahunna magical practice of Polynesia, these connection threads are treated almost physically, even with techniques for moving them from one place to another. If widespread belief in something is any indicator of truth (and it is not), the validity of the law of contagion can be considered proved.

It is the law of contagion which leads to the requirement in many spells for a piece of clothing or another personal possession of an individual to work magic against the person. In fact, it need not be a piece of clothing or intimate apparel. It is quite possible to work magic without this link at all. However, the link does provide a sort of "highway" from the magician to the intended subject of the operations.

There are ways of establishing this "highway" magically when it is not present. This is the method used by the "third party" magician who acts to quell battles between those who practice magic. The magician essentially ties each of the battling magicians in their own anger.

Images of people may be used in accordance with the law of contagion. Images, even as far away as fourth or fifth hand, will operate satisfactorily. Photographs are especially good for this purpose, as they are excellent transmitters of astral energies. Modern Polaroid photographs are such good energy transmitters that most people who have worked with them prefer them to anything else.

Articles of clothing are traditional items used for magical work, but in some cases, tools, jewelry and other personal possessions have been used. I have seen cases of dolls made and dressed up in a clothing made from the cast off clothing belonging to the person the spell was worked on. This is a very elaborate process, but it is quite effective.

By gaining an understanding of natural magic, and the rules of magical operations, we may come a great deal closer to our creator. Power, and the ability to perform magic, comes as the result of spiritual growth, never as the result of a desire for power—especially power over others. By practicing the exercises mentioned here, and by learning to place ourselves in harmony with the divine creation, through sincere reverence and respect for the creation, we can grow closer to God. It is this which gives us the right to practice natural magic.

Not in Conclusion

I say not in conclusion because there is no end to learning, especially in a field as diffuse and interesting as magic. Learning, in the sense of training our faculty for rational thought and developing our memory, is one of the chief goals of the process of education, and it plays a large part in our society. However, this kind of learning is only one kind of learning, and its nature limits our development when we accept it as our only means of acquiring knowledge.

We may say that we follow the principles of objective and scientific rational thought, as formulated by the learned sages of the past. In practice we find that our academic halls and universities are as much the victims of a social culture striving for individual gain, competition for reward, and as full of petty jealousy, as are the great debating societies of our democratic legislatures. This is only to be expected, as scholars and scientists in all fields are ultimately normal human beings. They have brought to their lofty academic positions all their internal tangled emotional baggage, and it is fully blended with their highly specialized technical educations.

Those who really have a desire and a drive to practice magic soon realize that they must first make something different of themselves, sharpening their natural tools and talents into something which is quite different than they can receive by participating in any program of formal academic education. I have mentioned that magic can never become a science. Indeed, it can only remain an art, an art which not all people can master. Having read through this book, you may now understand why I say that self-development, in the spiritual sense, must proceed mastering magical work in all cases.

Those who come to this Earth ready to practice magic are a rarity. As with natural talent in any other field, training in the practice of any art quickly allows those with no natural talent or inborn ability to surpass those who have been born with a natural talent or ability for the art. It is this training for magical practice that must be applied to develop any possible natural ability people may have.

In the various chapters of this book, beginning with chapter 2, I have attempted to indicate the lines of development that a person must follow to become a magician. If you take these exercises seriously, and work through them over a period of three or four years, you will find that your life will change for the better as you master these various exercises. The exercises promote changes which will take place even if you lose your initial interest in practicing magic.

This is one of the most interesting facets of the practice of magic. Going through the training required to practice magic gives you an entirely different vision of yourself – and the world around you – once the training itself is out of the way. It is much the same as training to be a member of any learned profession, in that the daily work of the profession is usually entirely different from the expectations which motivated the student to undertake to enter the profession. The day-to-day work of the average practicing attorney is far less interesting than the life of Perry Mason or any other courtroom television drama would have you believe. The same could be said for the day-to-day work of a physician or a professional engineer. It is the same with the day-to-day work of a magician, except that the training of a magician is properly directed toward harmonizing the self with the universe, rather than mastering a specific body of intellectual knowledge. Thus, when a magician has completed training he or she is in a different state. The magician has arrived at a place where mind, body and will operate together in a certain way. A trained magician is to some extent a changed person. The same is true of those martial arts experts who have really mastered their art. They develop into a kind of harmony with creation, something which is the real goal of human development.

For this reason there can be no conclusion, for either you will take advantage of the information in this book or you will not. If you do so, and follow at least some of the exercises given through to mastery, you will see your life change in interesting ways. If you do not take advantage of these exercises, you will find that the time will pass in any event. Your life will still encounter change, but not in the same way it would had you mastered the exercises given here. The real conclusion to this book is in your hands; you may do with it what you will.

Should you decide to follow these exercises and begin the long process of self-development which they entail, you will have aimed yourself toward one conclusion. If you do not, you will have aimed yourself toward another conclusion. Only you can decide which is ultimately the best conclusion for you.

As I said in the beginning, there is nothing particularly sacred or mysterious about the practice of magic, there is only a necessary training of the self, different from any intellectual training which you may be familiar with. It is the successful completion of this necessary training which makes a person a magician. The completely trained person is then able to practice any kind of magical mode they may desire.

Opportunities for self-delusion and deception are the constant companions of one who wishes to perform magic. Until a magician can be objective about his or her magical practice, and the results to be obtained from it, he or she can not be assured that the necessary level of consistency to accomplish everything he or she may desire has been reached. A good magician questions everything in a non-critical manner, and accepts only results that have been proven to exist physically as a result of his or her efforts. This requires that the magician keep good records of any magical work performed. Keeping an accurate magical diary, along the lines of the format shown below, is always a requirement for real success in magic. Keeping a diary of impressions and beliefs is not nearly as useful to your development. I recommend the following format:

Date of Operation:
Operation:
Date of Result:
Result:

Unfortunately, people who are self-deluded often keep a similar diary, entering their delusions about results as if it were the physical result. For those who do not delude themselves, practicing magic can be a great deal of fun, besides being personally rewarding. I prefer this objective approach, because I believe that living life requires a good sense of humor!

Appendix
The Emerald Tablet

This text was supposedly found in the tomb of Thrice Greatest Hermes, and was said to have been engraved on an emerald tablet. This text is often the first intimation concerning the correspondence between the physical and non-physical world that neophyte students receive from a teacher. The following is copied from the copy which I received from my teacher many years ago. I have no idea where he got it from, but I would assume it has been published in books from time to time.

True, without falsehood, certain and most true, that which is above is the same as that which is below, and that which is below is the same as that which is above, for the performance of the miracles of the One Thing. And as all Things are from One, by the mediation of One, so all things have their birth from this one thing by adaptation. The Sun is its Father the Moon is its Mother, the Wind carries it in its belly, its nurse is the Earth. This is the Father of all perfection, or consummation of the whole world. Its power is integrating, if it be turned into Earth.

You shall separate the Earth from the Fire, the subtle from the gross, suavely, and with great ingenuity and skill. Your skillful work ascends from Earth to Heaven, and descends again to Earth, and receives the power of the superiors and of the inferiors. So thou hast the glory of the whole world—therefore let all obscurity flee before thee. This is the strong force of all forces, overcoming every subtle and penetrating every solid thing. So all the world was created. Hence were all wonderful adaptations, of which this is the manner. Therefore I am called Hermes Trismegistus having three parts of the philosophy of the whole world. What I have to tell is completed concerning the operation of the Sun.[1]

---

[1]A slightly different version of this text is available in M. A. Atwood's *Hermetic Philosophy and Alchemy* (New York: Julian Press, 1960), p. 8.

Reading List

The following books are recommended to those who have an intellectual interest in magical practices, but who do not intend to master either magic or any specific magical practice.

Dancers to the Gods: The Magical Records of Charles Seymour and Christine Hartley. Edited and introduced by Alan Richardson. London: Aquarian Press, 1985. To be reissued as *The Magical Diaries of Dion Fortune.*

> This is the record of two ceremonial magicians of the English "changing the consciousness school." It makes interesting reading, but to me, it is not magic.

Natural Magick: The Magical State of Being. David Carroll and Barry Saxe. New York: Arbor House, 1977.

> An interesting book about the magical state of mind, with many examples of magicians, past and present.

Magic: An Occult Primer. David Conway. New York: E. P. Dutton, 1972. Now available from Aquarian Press (1987), a division of HarperCollins in London.

> This book is probably the best introduction to Ritual and Ceremonial Magic in the English language. As its title states, it is a primer of occult information concerning magic, with a definite bias toward ritual and ceremonial magic.

Experimental Magic. J. H. Brennan. London: Aquarian Press, 1972.

> This is another excellent introduction to the British version of ceremonial magic. Like the former work, it was written by a practicing magician.

The following books cover the history of the occult revival, and the many magical lodges of ritual and ceremonial magicians which derived from the revival of magic in Europe which followed the French Revolution.

The Rosy Cross Unveiled. Christopher McIntosh. London: Aquarian Press, 1980. Out of print.

> This book is a history of the Rosicrucian movement, which eventually gave birth to the magical revival. So far as it goes, this is probably the best non-specialist history of Rosicrucianism available. It is quite readable; many of the more ponderous histories are not.

Eliphas Levi and the French Occult Revival. Christopher McIntosh. New York: Samuel Weiser, 1972. Out of print.

> This book continues the story of the occult revival, from the time of the earliest cult founders in pre-revolutionary France to the odd people of the occult and their followers in the 1890s. It is an interesting book, as the author details many of these characters in a very clear light. It should be read by anyone interested in the history of the occult.

The Magicians of the Golden Dawn: A Documentary History of a Magical Order 1887–1923. Ellic Howe. York Beach, ME: Samuel Weiser, 1978; and Wellingborough, England: Aquarian Press, 1978. Out of print.

> Those who think that the Golden Dawn was the height of magical practice should read this book. The author documents his statements, taking them, for the most part, from the original sources. It is certainly an interesting text, and a most revealing history of this magical order.

There are a number of other books in this historical vein which could be cited, but as the above volumes all have bibliographies, and of the tracing of bibliographies there is no end, I will desist from listing more. I would encourage the reading of biographies rather than attempting to seek out strictly magical works, for understanding the lives of the magicians brings the reader an understanding of what real magic is, and exposes the causes of delusion.

The following books are listed as guides to training the mind. There are at least several hundred other worthwhile books that I have not listed, including Geofrey Leland's book on the Will. The few below will suffice to start students who wish to take the time to follow the directions given in them.

Concentration. Ernest Wood. Wheaton, IL: Quest, Theosophical Publishing House, 1949.

Concentration: A Guide to Mental Mastery. Mouni Sadhu. North Hollywood, CA: Wilshire Book Co., 1959.

Meditation. Mouni Sadhu. North Hollywood, CA: Wilshire Book Co., 1978.

The following books are mentioned in the text, and are cited here for general interest. Except for *Strange Experience*, the story of a real magician, these books are not recommended reading.

Strange Experience. Lee R. Gandee. Englewood Cliffs, NJ: Prentice Hall, 1971. Out of print.

Conjur Wife. Fritz Leiber. New York: Ace Books, 1981.

777 & Other Qabalistic Writings. Aleister Crowley. York Beach, ME: Samuel Weiser, 1970.

The Book of the Sacred Magic of Abra Melin, the Mage. Translated and edited by S. L. MacGregor-Mathers. New York: Causeway Books, 1974; New York: Dover, 1975.

Autobiography of Benvenuto Cellini (1500–1571). Translated by John A. Symonds. New York: Random House, Modern Library, 1985.

Secret Lodge. Cincinnati, OH: Black Moon Publishing Co., 1984, Archives FA #1.

> *Secret Lodge* is just one of the many classic publications available from the Archives of Black Moon Publishing Company, a clearinghouse for information on a variety of occult topics, primarily ceremonial magic. A list of their many publications is available, and students seriously interested in magic can

write to them for information. To get on their mailing list, send a SASE to: Archives, Black Moon Publishing Co., P. O. Box 19469, Cincinnati, OH 54219–0469.

Initiation into Hermetics. Franz Bardon. Wuppertal, Germany: Ruggeberg Verlag, 1962.

The Teachings of Don Juan. Carlos Castanada. New York: Pocket Books, 1990.

Medicine Woman. Lynn V. Andrews. San Francisco: HarperCollins, 1983.

Liber Kaos: The Psychonomicon. Peter J. Carroll. York Beach, ME: Samuel Weiser, 1992.

Index

Constantine, 27
conversion, 68, 69, 70
Conway, David, 50
Creator, 6, 11, 124, 135, 140, 145
Creator-Godhead, 28, 56
Crowley, Aleister, 12, 13, 37, 51, 117
cults, 57

D

Dancers to the Gods, 34
    working with, 82
death, 22, 81, 138, 144
Dee, Dr. John, 43
deity, 55, 56, 58, 62, 63, 64, 66, 69, 86, 101, 108, 117
    giving one's head to,
    Hebrew, 28
    seat of, 59
demons, 30
devil, 24, 28
dish, 102
divination, 45, 58, 64, 65, 77, 78, 85
diviner, 64, 65
"doll," 143
Don Juan, 67
drugs
    hallucinogenic, 34

E

Earth, 11, 21, 47, 58, 62, 87, 89, 91, 99, 125, 134, 147
Earth (element), 102, 106, 113, 114, 142
Eckan Kar, 86
Egypt, 79
"Eight," 45
elemental energies, 106
elemental forces, 102, 107
elementals, 30, 101

air, 108, 109
earth, 108, 109, 112
fire, 108, 109
water, 108
elements, 101, 103, 105, 106, 107, 111, 112, 113, 114, 126, 142
Emerald Tablet, 39
emotion, 4, 22
emotional catharsis, 16
emotional change, 16
emotional force, 3, 4, 17, 31
emotional level of being, 20
emotional nature, 17, 30
emotional trauma, 22
energy, 101, 136
    astral, 17, 18, 145
    emotional, 17, 18, 19, 30, 52
England, 81
Episcopal Church, 24
etheric projection, 85
Europe, 27
evil, 28
evil influences, 25
exorcisms, 23, 25
Extra Human Intelligences, 30

F

faith, 20, 46
    loss of, 21
"five element theory," 105
Fire, 102, 106, 113, 114, 141
flame, 102
Fludd, Robert, 118
Fortune, Dion, 6
funeral mass, 23

G

Gandee, Lee R. 31
God, 20, 21, 29, 41, 69, 101, 117, 134, 137, 145
gods, 101

About the Author

Draja Mickaharic was born in rural Bosnia just before the First World War. He immigrated to the United States in 1939, and practiced as a magician, referring to himself as a witchdoctor, for forty-five years. Now retired from active practice, he devotes his time to writing and counseling his few students who still actively work in the field. He is the author of two books also published by Samuel Weiser: *Spiritual Cleansing*, published in 1982, and *Century of Spells*, published in 1988.